The Challenge to
Higher Education

Titles recently published under the SRHE/Open University Press imprint:

Michael Allen: *The Goals of Universities*
William Birch: *The Challenge to Higher Education*
Heather Eggins: *Restructuring Higher Education*
Colin Evans: *Language People*
Gunnar Handal and Per Lauvås: *Promoting Reflective Teaching*
Vivien Hodgson *et al*: *Beyond Distance Teaching, Towards Open Learning*
Peter Linklater: *Education and the World of Work*
Graeme Moodie: *Standards and Criteria in Higher Education*
John Pratt and Suzanne Silverman: *Responding to Constraint*
Marjorie E. Reeves: *The Crisis in Higher Education*
John T. E. Richardson: *Student Learning*
Derek Robbins: *The Rise of Independent Study*
Gordon Taylor *et al*: *Literacy by Degrees*
Malcolm Tight: *Academic Freedom and Responsibility*
Alan Woodley *et al*: *Choosing to Learn*

The Challenge to Higher Education:

Reconciling Responsibilities to Scholarship and to Society

William Birch

The Society for Research into Higher Education &
Open University Press

Published by SRHE and
Open University Educational Enterprises Limited
12 Cofferidge Close
Stony Stratford
Milton Keynes MK11 1BY, England

and
242 Cherry Street
Philadelphia, PA 19106, USA

First Published 1988

British Library Cataloguing in Publication Data

Birch, William
   The challenge to higher education:
   reconciling responsibilities to scholarship
   and to society.
   1. Great Britain. Higher education
   I. Title   II. Society for Research into
   Higher Education
   378.41

   ISBN 0-335-09519-4

Library of Congress Cataloging-in-Publication Data

Birch, William
   The challenge to higher education:
reconciling responsibilities to scholarship
   and society / William Birch.
   p.   cm. — (SRHE monograph)
   Bibliography: p.
   Includes index.
   1. Education, Higher—Great Britain—
Evaluation.   2. Education, Higher—Social aspects—
Great Britain.   I. Title   II. Series: Research into
higher education monographs
LA637.B57   1988
378.41—dc 19   88-22394 CIP

ISBN 0-335-09519-4

Typeset by Rowland Phototypesetting Limited
Bury St Edmunds, Suffolk
Printed in Great Britain by St Edmundsbury Press Limited
Bury St Edmunds, Suffolk

Contents

Preface

This book has been written in part as a means to reflecting on a varied, interesting and valued career in higher education in Britain, the United States and Canada. However, the more basic purpose is to try to demonstrate the need for higher education in Britain to examine itself more critically, to review and update the presuppositions which underpin its roles in research and education, and to assume itself, where possible, the initiative for dealing with the conclusions. What I have to say does not constitute in any sense a comprehensive review. However, the challenge which is identified and discussed appears to be central to the urgent process of reappraisal and adjustment which higher education in Britain needs to undergo. If the book is able to contribute to the sense of urgency, to the necessary sense of problem; and if, above all, it can assist in bringing about constructive change, I shall be delighted.

My own credentials are primarily experiential. They reflect a career in which a concern for policy matters, from the scale of the department to that of the institution and the system itself, have always vied with my interests in properly scholarly activities! The great majority of these years were spent in university life: ten years as a lecturer in Bristol; three as a professor in the Graduate School of Geography in Clark University, Worcester, Massachusetts; four as Professor and Chairman of the Department of Geography in the University of Toronto; and eight years as Professor and Head of the Department of Geography in the University of Leeds. These immensely enjoyable years gave me great respect for the high scholarly standards and commitment of most colleagues and an understanding of the variety and depth of the intellectual resources available in a university. I was, however, surprised and saddened by what seemed to be overly inward-looking attitudes and at times complacency.

In Bristol University I was glad, therefore, to have a small role in hosting the British Association for the Advancement of Science in 1955; and valued enormously the interaction it provided with other fields of research and learning and with participants from outside university life. Likewise, in my own early research into the geographical adjustments involved in the evolution of the economy of the Isle of Man (Birch, 1961), I was impressed by the richness of the interface between geography and the world of affairs and the opportunity which it provided to explore the meaning of strategic thinking and planning.

Clark University, a small privately funded liberal arts college plus a graduate school, was an impressive institution both intellectually and socially. The influence of its President, Howard B. Jefferson, was immense. Jefferson was a big man in all respects and a distinguished scholar. He presided, in what would now be described as a paternal style, over the scholarly and administrative life of the university. He was ambitious for Clark and worked hard in close contact with staff to explain and to develop his sense of the future. Howard Jefferson was a resolute yet humane leader of the type which it seems to me has an enduring role in the affairs of higher education. An anecdote is illustrative of the man and his university. At Christmas time, the Jeffersons gave a party for the staff in their rambling, white colonial house on campus. I recall sitting down to join a more elderly man playing chess – and, of course, enquired in due course 'What is your subject?' He replied easily and with a smile, 'I am the gardener'. Jefferson's university was intellectually élite but not socially élite.

The large, diverse and generally distinguished University of Toronto was, in the 1960s, leading and enjoying leading the expansion of graduate education in Ontario. It was served by some very able people. Vincent Bladen, a Balliol economist of high standing, and again a man of great humanity and force of personality, was my immediate and genial superior as Dean of the large Faculty of Arts (Science was an unstated part of the Faculty!). Faculty Boards were concerned with shaping policy – with essentially strategic considerations. The Dean and his two Associates (a philosopher and a chemist) were concerned to ensure that well-considered actions were taken at the departmental level in the implementation of policy. To this end, departments had great freedom of action, with budgets which were comprehensive, including provision for salaries. Both annually and as required by departmental or deanly initiative, Vincent Bladen and his colleagues conducted a rigorous examination of departmental proposals with the Chairman and a small group of colleagues – but it was the Chairman's grasp of things that was being tested. If satisfied, they provided their backing and encouragement. Alternatively one's failure was explained. Succeeding with Vincent Bladen depended on prior detailed and close examination with colleagues of the policy arguments being advanced; and it was clear in Toronto that the distinguished departments were by and large those which were highly interactive and carefully planned.

In the University of Leeds, as in Toronto, Geography had fallen behind. However, the decision-making context within which the problem had to be addressed was very different. Leeds was a highly centralized university in which much authority was vested in a small group of senior committees of the Senate, chaired by the Vice-Chancellor. One's good fortune in being appointed or elected to a number of these committees provided the opportunity to establish (or to undermine!) one's own credibility and that of the claims of the department. The judgements made by committees of peers were inevitably more 'political' than those in the highly rational, executive system in Toronto. However, the situation was both instructive and challenging. As Vice-Chancellor, Lord Boyle developed the University further as a lively and agreeable place, and identified closely with the pure academic ethic. This ethic was surprisingly strong in Leeds, given its substantial concern with technological and medical education. It was reflected in its relationships within the region and not least in its attitudes towards the colleges of education, the new Leeds Polytechnic and the University of Bradford. I recall sitting, as the social scientist, on the committee concerned with the award of higher doctorates and being struck by the values presupposed in the tendency for pure academic criteria to be applied, sometimes rather awkwardly, to evidently distinguished work in technological fields, where much of the achievement had lain in testing, extending and applying basic knowledge and the theoretical gain was therefore more normative than fundamental.

Discussion with colleagues in Toronto and Leeds led to the conviction that much of the theoretical and practical gain in Geography, both in research and learning, was to be found in its contact with policy matters: with urban, regional and natural resource planning. Whilst in Toronto, I had been much influenced by the arguments of Edward Shils that the social sciences would benefit at this stage in their development from a stronger and more explicit problem-orientation. I was also struck by Michael Polanyi's writing on the theory of problem-based enquiry. These experiences emphasized further my interests in what I have come to call the operational dimension of research and learning – that which is concerned explicitly with the relationship between knowledge and action in the world of affairs. The term 'operational' itself emphasizes the connection with action – with achieving change. It is thus more general and useful than the terms 'applied' and 'vocational', each of which has also acquired adverse connotations in academic circles.

Experiences in North America and in Leeds, coupled with a continuing zest for involvement in policy-making in higher education (strengthened and sharpened through working with Edward Boyle) were largely responsible for my taking an active interest in the emergence of the polytechnics – aided by those accomplished persuaders, Alex Smith and Patrick Nuttgens. During my twelve years as Director of Bristol Polytechnic, I found great interest and satisfaction with colleagues in extending further its interaction with the regional socio-economic community, and in developing a strong teaching and a growing research and consultancy role. This role covered a wide range of essentially operational fields, which were supported by basic strength in the sciences, social sciences and humanities. With the benefit of university experience, I was able to satisfy myself that properly conducted operational learning and research are no less demanding than their basic academic counterparts, and may for many students be more stimulating. It was an important part of my concern and responsibility in Bristol Polytechnic to move it towards a more fully participative concern with policy-making at all levels in the institution, in the belief that this would release additional initiative and creative energy. In so doing, I am not sure, on reflection, that I observed sufficiently carefully lessons learned elsewhere, namely, the importance of clarifying the realms of policy-making and executive action in order to ensure not only that policy can be shaped through the search for consensus but that action can be taken expeditiously. It is an issue which is of some importance in a period of retrenchment and restructuring in higher education within which the balance between the 'political' and the rational content of governance requires particularly close attention.

An important source of the danger of undue politicization in the polytechnics has arisen from their enforced intimacy with local government and therefore with a system which appears all too often to be about power rather than principle. This was evident to me as Chairman of the Committee of Directors of Polytechnics (CDP), at the time when the National Advisory Body (NAB) was in its early days. The NAB was an essentially political device to appease the local authority associations. Its structure was also political, being designed to ensure that the local authority members of the Superior Committee exercised effective control. Yet it was already abundantly clear on grounds of efficiency of operation, let alone the prevention of political interference, that the polytechnics needed to be given corporate status and brought into the overall strategic planning of higher education.

I was fortunate in the later years of my period at Bristol Polytechnic to be granted study leave and to receive sponsorship for two overseas lecture and seminar tours, in Scandinavia, Western Europe, North America, Japan, Hong Kong, Singapore and Australia. My purpose was to explore approaches in other countries to strengthening the operational dimension of research and learning. I was also concerned to explore experiments in problem-based learning and their relationship to a more purposive approach to study in both the basic disciplines and operational fields. A report was submitted to the Department of Education and Science, my main sponsor, under the title *An Enquiry into the Changing Relationship between Higher Education and Society*, and this book draws heavily on the report.

It has been possible during the past two years, whilst enjoying a Visiting Professorship in the Institute of Education of the University of London, to relate experience more effectively to the substantial literature in higher education. However, in writing this book I have not sought to present a balanced appraisal. The account is an essentially personal one designed to raise questions and, if possible, to stimulate further enquiry into the presuppositions which inform our sense of purpose in higher education and into the approaches which we might adopt more effectively to further this sense of purpose.

I have received valuable criticism and advice from Mary Birch, Sinclair Goodlad, Graham Haydon, Paul Hirst, Pauline Perry and Gareth Williams. I wish to thank them most warmly and of course to exonerate them.

Introduction and Summary

In discussing *The Concept of the Mind*, Ryle (1949) found it necessary to observe that '. . . theorists have been so pre-occupied with investigating the nature, the source and the credentials of the theories that we adopt that they have for the most part ignored the question, what it is for someone to know how to perform tasks.' Scholarship is properly concerned with the development and the validation of theories which 'explain' the world in which we live and the way in which we behave in dealing with that world and with each other. This basic, intrinsic purpose is essential; but it should be capable also of enriching and being enriched by the grasp which society has of the practical problems – the tasks – which it has to discharge. However, the natural drives of scholarship towards statements at the most general level, if not coupled with a concern to draw out (and where necessary research into) the implications for the operational needs of society, create a serious gap in understanding and communication. I shall argue that closing, or at least narrowing, this gap represents the outstanding challenge to higher education – a challenge which has meaning at all levels of scale and for most activities.

I share the view, developed by Argyris (1982) and others that insufficient interaction across such a gap, and therefore between theory and action, sets serious limitations to the achievable basic understanding of the real worlds of nature and human affairs as well as limiting unnecessarily the basis for policy-making and action. Scott (1984) has I believe pointed to an important part of the general problem:

> Britain has only the most vestigial intelligentsia because the main role of an intelligentsia is to communicate academic learning in a sensible way to society at large, a role that is barely recognised in Britain . . . So in Britain we have the clear paradox: a higher education system of considerable academic brilliance, and a society sunk deeper in philistinism, suspicious of new ideas and scornful of rationality. Both go their own way. Both lose.

I am not unmindful of the importance in higher education of creative tension of the type implied in Smelser's (1973) observation:

> . . . the educational system stands continuously in a state of precarious
> balance and potential conflict over different priorities: to what extent
> should it be expected to maximise its own values of cognitive rationality
> (generating knowledge, searching for truths, teaching and learning in the
> broadest sense) and to what extent should it be required to 'service' the
> values and needs of other sectors of society? This question is the subject of
> continuous uncertainty and conflict. Since higher education serves many
> masters, including itself, it is to be expected that it stands on the precipice
> of value conflicts at all times.

However, value conflicts have become unduly divisive in English higher
education and are, in my view, undermining both achievement and recognition
by opening up an unnecessarily wide gap, both within the system and between
scholarship and society.

This book is concerned, therefore, to identify the sources of the challenge
which has been adduced, to examine the issues of value and purpose in
education and research that require reappraisal if the challenge is to be met, and
to set out a framework for replanning and managing higher education – one
which is capable of dealing effectively with the challenge.

The first chapter outlines the history of what are referred to as the closed-
system tendencies in higher education – the propensities to operate largely from
internally generated stimuli and to validate the responses within the relatively
closed circle of international scholarship. This intrinsic life of higher education
is important in its own right, in so far as it provides the essential conditions for a
detached and critical approach both to scholarship and to society. However, its
importance is diminished and its public position endangered if it fails to take an
active interest in, to enrich and be enriched by, the world of policy and practical
affairs. Successive failures on the part of higher education itself, as well as
government and its agencies, to come to terms with this requirement are
examined, with the conclusions that: the role of higher education as a public
service should be reappraised, that the traditional academic ethic should be
rethought and broadened, and that the system of higher education as a whole
should be replanned in order to ensure an appropriate response.

In discussing, in the third chapter, the position of higher education as a public
service, further attention is given to reconciling this position with the needs of
scholarship, with the conclusion that on balance there are clear advantages for
both scholarship and society. However, in order to seek some clarification of the
meaning both of autonomy and accountability, the essential conditions for
achieving an appropriate balance are examined.

The central question of the values and sense of purpose in research and
learning which inform the academic ethic is the subject of the fourth chapter. It
examines the strengths and the limitations of the traditional academic ethic –
that which relates back to the closed-system tendencies and to misgivings about
engagement with the world of affairs as a public service. Arguments are
advanced, at the level of both principle and practice, for a broader conception of
the academic ethic within which the basic academic disciplines are brought into

more fruitful and systematic interaction with operational fields of knowledge – those fields (the technologies and the older and newer learned professions) within which the essential purpose is both to create knowledge and put it to work in addressing intellectually demanding practical problems. The implications of such a broadened academic ethic for research are examined, with the following conclusions: that the research community should be expected to show, and would itself benefit from showing, a greater concern for the operational significance of research and particularly for strategic problems at the interface between basic research and prospective technological advances; that research consultancy in outside organizations should be actively encouraged; and that there should be a revision of the arrangements for setting research priorities and a more selective approach to research funding above a general threshold level.

In examining, in the fifth chapter, the educational implications of a broader conception of the academic ethic, attention is given to analysing the conditions necessary for a liberal and general education and for one that has a purposive thrust. It is possible to point to considerable theoretical and practical difficulties in the undue and restrictive academicism associated with specialized Honours degree courses derived from the basic academic disciplines, and related closely to the value system of the traditional academic ethic. Such courses neither provide for a truly liberal approach to undergraduate education, nor do they facilitate the development of the general and transferable intellectual skills, the achievement of which is the essential mark of intellectual excellence. Arguments are advanced to show that such general intellectual skills come into play and are developed most readily in an interdisciplinary context – one given focus and coherence by the identification of themes and problems which have both theoretical and practical significance. Such problems may have theoretical implications of a sufficient scale to require a dominant concern with the relevant basic disciplines. However, problems of equivalent intellectual weight also exist in regard to the operational fields of study and research, and their pursuit is capable of enriching both theory and practice. Indeed, it is possible to argue that the models for learning, and in particular the problem-based models, current in some of the technologies and the learned professions, have meaning for approaches in higher education generally. This is so because they address more directly and successfully the issue of developing general and transferable intellectual skills. It is also so because they provide a more purposive and structured approach which is capable of lifting the threshold level of attainment in mass higher education as well as exciting the interest and motivation of the most able students – the source of Ashby's (1974) '. . . thin clear stream of excellence.' Such excellence would also be encouraged, and a wider range of choices offered to both full-time and part-time students, by the adoption of a two-plus-two structure of undergraduate study – generally accessible Pass degree courses followed by more specialized Honours courses for those reaching an appropriate standing. This arrangement would have the additional merit of increasing effectiveness in the use of scarce resources.

The realization of the intellectual substance of a broader academic ethic, and the research and learning which it is capable of generating, is dependent on the achievement of a more interactive relationship between higher education and the world of affairs. The sixth chapter is, therefore, devoted to an examination of the means to greater interaction at the system, institutional, departmental and individual levels, both within higher education and between it and industry, commerce, the professions and the public service. Examples are given of the successful development of regional and national networks of interaction within a range of countries visited during two periods of study leave, with particular reference to Scandinavia and North America.

Thoughts on a more open and interactive system of higher education – one embracing a broader view of the academic ethic and having a more purposive thrust in learning – are not new. They are rather a restatement of the educational philosophy of Dewey (1916) and others and therefore have long-standing. This pragmatic philosophy appears to be closely consistent with public expectations of higher education and to some extent with the current thrust of government policies. It is also consistent with the position of many younger academics, who are at once seized by the responsibilities of scholarship and by the responsibility of giving such intellectual leadership as may be possible towards the solution of pressing problems within a troubled society. A relatively extreme view of such a position is given by Maxwell (1984) in his stimulating book, *From Knowledge to Wisdom*: 'Far from giving priority to problems of knowledge, inquiry must . . . give absolute priority to the intellectual tasks of articulating our problems, proposing and criticizing possible solutions, possible and actual human *actions*.'

However, the conception of a broader academic ethic which is developed appears to be at variance with that still prevailing in many of our leading institutions of higher education. At their core, such institutions retain an ethos which is essentially traditional; and this is reflected in much research and teaching. Moves to interact more seriously with the extrinsic sources of insight and stimulus appear all too often to represent a somewhat grudging response to the pressures of financial retrenchment, rather than in principle concern to recognize and to meet the challenge which has been identified in this book. There are of course important exceptions in British higher education and they point the way encouragingly.

The final chapter underlines, however, the fact that the achievement of a more interactive system of higher education within a more broadly conceived academic ethic would require considerable change and adjustment. Such change will not be achieved sufficiently quickly or fully through exhortation nor through the operation of the relatively imperfect market forces which arise from competition between sectors and institutions. The importance to the national interest – in both research and education – of achieving a substantial measure of change and adjustment argues for the creation of a strategic planning body for higher education as a whole, with a substantial degree of statutory independence but correspondingly well-established modes of accountability. The conception and relatively simple structure of such a body are examined. Its role is discussed in relation to the creation of an integrated system of higher education within which the notion of a broader academic ethic and a more purposive, basic and operational, approach to research and education would find particular expression in perhaps twenty major research universities, created through the merger and internal rationalization of the older and some of the newer civic universities and adjacent polytechnics – such universities would have major Extension Divisions for part-time education within their general regions. This group would include Oxford and Cambridge and federal institutions within the conurbations of London, Manchester and Birmingham. A further group of about twenty smaller universities with more limited research funding would be created from the remaining universities and polytechnics, with some mergers of adjacent institutions. The role, in higher education, of the colleges of higher education and the colleges of further education would require radical re-appraisal, for the latter group in relation to the role of the Extension Divisions of major research universities. This chapter gives consideration finally to the implications of a strategically planned and integrated system of higher education for the roles of institutions and their effective leadership and management, and for the operation of the academic profession.

In the present relatively unplanned system of higher education within which rather ill-defined notions of autonomy and academic freedom often appear to weigh more heavily than securing clear and significant national objectives, considerable resistance and even resentment might be anticipated for the proposals which this book seeks to advance. However, it is important to be clear that, although higher education in Britain has in general enjoyed a secure and esteemed place within the social and intellectual fabric, this situation is not unchanging and does indeed appear to have deteriorated. A positive concern therefore on the part of higher education itself to think through and, where necessary, research into the requirements for ensuring a more purposive response to the challenge outlined, may in the end be the most certain way of securing the conditions necessary for effective support and for an appropriate autonomy.

1

Closed-system Tendencies in Higher Education

The most basic consideration underlying the emergence of the current challenge to higher education, to reconcile more effectively its responsibilities to scholarship and to society, is its inherent tendency to behave as a relatively closed academic system. That is to say, the systems of relationships which arise through scholarly activity are to a substantial degree internal to the community of scholars, in its various forms, and are capable of being energized (fed by stimuli and responses) from within that community without necessary reference to the world of affairs. In other words, the concept of an ivory tower has a substantive as well as a symbolic significance. It also has a lengthy history.

The classical distinction between speculative reason and practical reason is central to the notion of the academy and its concern with the pursuit of knowledge for its own sake. Such a pursuit of essentially theoretical understanding was held to be capable of providing at once a grasp of the essential nature of things and a means, through the development of the intellect, to the achievement of the whole person. In consequence, it was held to be the appropriate means to educating the ruling class. This élite and detached view of the pursuit of pure knowledge and learning remains an important support of the sense of values and purpose which inform higher education, at least in the western world. Minogue (1973) has restated this view:

> Knowledge is an understanding of the principle of things, and is composed of clear ideas or forms from which the accidental and contingent associations inevitably found in the world are purged.

It is a remarkable testimony to the strength of this position among scholars that the relatively closed notion of the academy has persisted to a marked degree, in a world beset by increasingly complex and serious problems.

The emergence of the university in mediaeval Europe, as a physical and social expression of the scholarly community, was closely associated with the Church and with the preparation of students for the learned professions: law, medicine and the Church. Cobham (Perkin, 1984) refers to them as '. . . primarily vocational schools for the professions, affording only a minimal expression for the concept of study *per se*.' The eventual and difficult separation of these universities from the Church was a notable contribution to the ethos of higher education, in the sense that it was a search for the freedom to pursue the truth unfettered by the dogma and therefore the constraints of the Church. The difficulty with which this necessary detachment was achieved may have contributed to the growth within higher education itself of a dogma that academic freedom is in all respects an absolute – a dogma which has contributed significantly to the excesses of the closed-system view.

Within the western tradition of scholarship and learning, the emphasis on the pursuit of knowledge for its own sake and, therefore, in detachment from the world of affairs, was given powerful stimulus by developments in Prussia in the early nineteenth century. These developments were associated particularly with the work of Wilhelm von Humboldt in Berlin who established the rationale of the research university, based on the assumption of a creative interplay between research and student learning. The basic argument is unexceptionable and has underpinned the quality of higher education and the growth of knowledge. However, in its more extreme forms the research university has given rise, as Scott (1984) has observed, to a rather 'retreatist' academicism, which has been a powerful force in developing closed-system tendencies.

British reaction to the notion of the research university was slow: until the developing strength of the research-oriented natural sciences was brought to bear; until Oxford and Cambridge began to respond under the pressure of informed opinion and government action; and until the first civic universities were established in the nineteenth century. Hitherto, greater emphasis was placed on a more limited and essentially humane view of scholarship and on the importance of teaching and learning within this context. The classical notion of the development of the rounded and liberally-educated person was thus carried forward and found fruitful expression in the Oxbridge tutorial system. As Ashby (1958) observed:

> Prominent among [the] assumptions in Oxford and Cambridge was a belief that the university existed to produce servants for church and state – cultivated men but not intellectuals. It was more important for university graduates to be civilized than learned . . . liberal education . . . rather than vocational training was the responsibility of the university.

There is, of course, the implication that a concern with practical matters (irrespective of other intellectual demands) is inherently uncivilizing – like trade! Barnett (1979) and others have drawn attention to the importance of this exclusive set of beliefs and values on the whole of the British educational system, and thus on British society generally and its attitude to practical affairs, including the creation and the distribution of wealth.

The ethos of the liberal university was codified by the writing of Cardinal Newman (1852):

> This process . . . by which the intellect, instead of being formed or sacrificed to some particular, accidental purpose, some specific trade or profession, or study or science, is disciplined for its own sake, for the perception of its proper object and for its own highest culture is called Liberal Education.

Newman envisaged research being pursued in a separate academy, in order that the university might concentrate on the achievement of the liberally-educated student–dons needed to be above all cultivated scholars in order to induct undergraduates into the values appropriate to a civilized life and leadership. This collegial and cloistering emphasis within British higher education is itself an expression of the relatively closed-system view and remains strongly established.

Scott (1984) has argued that:

> The liberal university saw its responsibility as to reproduce professions, but professions defined as much by social custom as by technological requirement, and to transmit cultural capital in its broadest sense and perhaps most metaphysical sense by the formation of élites. As a result, the liberal university distrusted vocationalism and technology and often appeared alienated from the values of industrial society.

It is not surprising, therefore, that the entry of technological research and learning into the university was resisted, notwithstanding the fact that Britain, through the initiative of relatively unschooled but brilliant craftsmen-inventor-entrepreneurs, was currently leading the industrial revolution, and displayed its achievements in the Great Exhibition of 1851. Technological education at a higher level awaited the introduction into schooling by the 1870s of a serious concern with science, associated with the influence of the Prince Consort and the establishment of a government department of Science and Art. Even so, it was found necessary to refer to the relevant Select Committee as being concerned with '. . . the Provisions for giving Instruction in Theoretical and Applied Science to the Industrial Classes' (Ashby, 1958).

Cumulatively, sufficient pressure was generated and conviction developed for the universities to open themselves to research and instruction in the technologies. Government support, arising from a growing concern over industrial competition and over issues of national security, was a major consideration. It is significant of the strength of the liberal ethic in the universities and its acceptance within established society that, in Britain, technological education was not initially segregated within new and separate institutions. The view was taken that, 'The manager-technologist must receive not only a vocational training: he must also enjoy the benefits of a liberal education; or at least he must rub shoulders with students who are studying the humanities' (Ashby, 1958). From all points of view, the inclusion of the technologies within the universities was evidently a correct decision, albeit one taken substantially out of self-interest by the universities.

However, the universities' belief in the pure academic ethic, the pervasive 'Oxbridge' tradition of educating civilized thinkers rather than 'doers', the underpinning of the 'Oxbridge' ethic by that of the public schools, and perhaps the lack of a serious concern among most industrialists at that stage with the value of higher education, did not provide the most appropriate context for the technologies to flourish. Indeed, it is clear that the concern of the universities with the basic disciplines, including the increasingly influential natural sciences, distorted the growth of technological education and research. The new operational fields of study were expected to prove themselves as respectable research and teaching disciplines, within the set of basic academic values established particularly by the natural sciences. They were therefore handicapped in developing programmes of research and teaching of the type needed by industry and the world of affairs generally. The relatively closed system of the universities had thus protected itself by accepting the technologies and acculturating them. Butterfield, a humanist, and for a period the Vice-Chancellor of Cambridge, found it possible to write, as late as 1961, that:

> The problem of technology involves some delicate issues. One man [who seems to be in a position to know about these matters] holds the view that it is better to have a good chemist and a good engineer than to have two chemical engineers. The former will knock sparks off one another and reach something novel, he says, while the minds of the latter will have been channelled too early into appointed grooves.

Lest Butterfield's observation appear to be an unduly partial one, it is valuable to quote again from Ashby (1958), a natural scientist and a great believer in the importance of the universities' concern with the technologies:

> And so the crude engineer and the mere technologist [the very adjectives are symptoms of the attitude] are tolerated in universities because the state and industry are willing to pay for them. Tolerated but not assimilated; for the traditional don is not yet willing to admit that technologists may have anything intrinsic to contribute to academic life. It is not yet taken for granted that a faculty of technology enriches a university intellectually as well as materially.

In my own university of the 1950s, Bristol, already distinguished in the natural sciences and the humanities, the faculty of engineering still languished 'down the hill' in the outmoded building of the college founded by the Society of Merchant Venturers prior to the establishment of the university. In a more general context, Snow (1961) bemoaned the relative failure of the civic universities to take seriously the needs of industry and of the cities that lobbied for and sponsored their creation:

> Almost none of the talent, almost none of the imaginative energy went back into the [industrial] revolution that was producing wealth. The traditional culture became more abstracted from it as it became more wealthy, trained its young men for administration, for the Indian Empire, for the purpose of penetrating the culture, but never in any circumstances to equip them to understand the revolution or take part in it.

The Imperial College of Science and Technology was founded at the turn of the century; but by this time, according to Barnett (1979), 'Germany possessed ten technical high schools of university rank with some 14,000 students.' He notes the success of these institutions in Germany by the time of the First World War, and draws out important consequences both for the conduct of the war and for the future of British industry.

In the immediate aftermath of the First World War, the University Grants

Committee (UGC) was established 'To enquire into the financial needs of University Education in the United Kingdom and to advise the Government as to the application of any grants that may be made.' The absence of any reference to the purpose of higher education and its relationship to national needs is an interesting reflection of government's tacit acceptance of the relatively closed-system mode of operation, its sense of purpose and the implications for policy. It is a comment also on, what Scott (1984) has described as the high degree of mutual trust between the universities and the politico-governmental establishment – a situation which has perhaps led to the universities being insufficiently self critical.

During the Second World War, the need for the urgent application of research to matters of national security and the insatiable demand for people educated and in some cases technically-trained for leadership, brought about a remarkable opening out of higher education. The results were in many ways impressive. However, Barnett (1987) has shown that the besetting problem of a relatively closed system of higher education, namely, a disinclination actively to relate theory to practice, resulted in an immensely serious problem of technological transfer, as between the scientists and the production process.

The pent-up demand for higher education, resulting from six years of war, was given permanent expression by the introduction of universal secondary education in the Education Act of 1944. The establishment in 1961 of the Robbins enquiry into *Higher Education* (1962) was a necessary consequence. The Committee was charged:

> . . . to review the pattern of full-time higher education in Great Britain and in the light of national needs and resources to advise Her Majesty's Government on what principles its long-term development should be based. In particular, to advise, in the light of these principles, whether there should be any changes in that pattern, whether any new types of institution are desirable and whether any modifications should be made in the present arrangements for planning and co-ordinating the development of the various types of institution.

The Report itself shows a clear appreciation of both the social and the economic arguments for the principle that admission to courses of higher education '. . . should be available for all those qualified by ability and attainment to pursue them and who wish to do so'. It noted that:

> The extension of educational opportunity in the schools and the widening of the desire for higher education on the part of young people have greatly increased the demand for places. At the same time, the growing realisation of this country's dependence upon the education of its population has led to much questioning of the adequacy of the present arrangements. Unless higher education is speedily reformed . . . there is little hope of this densely populated island maintaining an adequate position in the fiercely competitive world of the future.

However, while providing a formidable rationale for progress towards the more muted British version of what has come to be known as 'mass higher education',

Robbins failed to think through the serious implications for teaching and research and for the nature and the structure of the system, *qua* system, of higher education that would need to emerge. The Report recognized that student motivation for learning and excelling would be associated increasingly with individual judgements on the potential implications for success and satisfaction in the world of work: '. . . we deceive ourselves if we claim that more than a small fraction of students . . . would be where they are if there were no significance for their future careers and it is a mistake to suppose that there is anything discreditable about this.' The Report also noted the limitations (and the strengths), in a more open admissions context, of the specialized, single subject Honours degree and argued for broader and in that sense more general degree courses. Robbins affirmed the basic importance of undergraduates developing their general qualities of mind – those which imply intellectual skills capable of transcending the immediate referends of both subject matter and problem. Thus, the Committee observed, somewhat self-consciously: '. . . it is the distinguishing characteristic of a healthy higher education that *even* [my italics] where it is concerned with practical techniques, it imparts them on a plane of generality that makes possible their application to many problems – to find the one in the many, the general characteristic in the collection of particulars. It is this that the world of affairs demands of the world of learning.'

However, although the 'Aims and Principles' of the Report were far-sighted, it is now evident that Robbins, and the universities in their response to Robbins, failed seriously to come to terms with the requirements of mass higher education. In particular, they failed to make sufficient provision for the acquisition of truly general intellectual skills and the capacity to put them to work in addressing problems both in the basic disciplines and in the operational fields of study – operational in the sense that knowledge is sought with a view to action. This failure lies at the centre of higher education's continuing difficulty in discharging successfully its two-fold responsibilities to scholarship and to the wider needs of society. This difficulty is evident in research as well as in teaching undergraduates. It appears to be a reflection of a deep-seated concern to preserve the traditional, relatively closed system conception of higher education based on its capacity to generate and validate its activities without serious reference to extrinsic considerations – based also on dogmatic rather than reasoned considerations of autonomy. I recall the extraordinary anxieties of the University of Bristol in addressing the question of growth – by later standards very modest growth. The sense of opportunity presented by the prospect of growth was overpowered by a concern to preserve the *status quo*, seen as necessary to a defence both of standards and of autonomy. How very different was one's experience working in immediately subsequent years in graduate and undergraduate universities in the United States and Canada. Opportunities were seized with a sense of adventure, with confidence that research and teaching could benefit and with vigilance in maintaining the conditions necessary for an appropriate autonomy. Scott (1984) has summarized the British situation very effectively in commenting quite properly on the substantial achievements of the Robbins Report:

The great expansion in the number of students and increase in the number
of university institutions was undoubtedly a considerable achievement.
But it was also a controlled achievement in the sense that its effects were
carefully contained. The development of the universities stopped short of
that point beyond which fundamental questions would have to be asked
about the purpose of university education.

In the aftermath of Robbins, the universities' severely 'contained' view of their
national purpose was evident in the failure of the UGC and the CVCP, in their
advice to government, to ensure that, as a general solution, the translation into
universities of the Colleges of Advanced Technology (CATs) carried forward
the important tradition of part-time education and open interaction with the
regional socio-economic communities. An important, strategic opportunity was
lost to bring within the scope of the UGC, and therefore of unified planning for
higher education, the particular responsibilities for developing technological
and other operational forms of research and teaching on an equal basis of
support and esteem with pursuits in the basic disciplines. As with technological
subjects in the nineteenth century, so with the new technological universities,
the university community absorbed and acculturated them within the traditional
academic ethic, without evident hindrance from government which had created
and defined the role of the CATs. The continuing strength of the narrow value
assumptions on the part of the UGC in dealing with the technological universities was evident in the disproportionate share of financial retrenchment borne by
a number of them in 1981. Ashworth (1982) noted that: '. . . almost the only
positive "advice" the UGC letter contained was a suggestion that Salford University should go ahead with the establishment of an English Degree and afford
special protection to Economics and Geography – in a technological university;
in the middle of the worst recession to hit the country for half a century.'

The commitment of the university community to a relatively closed definition
of the set of relationships with which it should properly be concerned, and the set
of values which this commitment presupposes, was evident in the way that the
universities stood back from and even carped at the creation of the polytechnics
in the late 1960s – and thereby the creation of a clumsy, inefficient and
politically fraught binary system. How refreshing it would have been in the
national interest – and how sensible it would have been in securing relatively
autonomous control of additional resources and opportunities – if the UGC and
the CVCP had exerted themselves to secure a thorough review of the way in
which basic academic considerations and pressing operational needs could be
sensibly related within an integrated system of higher education. The White
Paper, A Plan for Polytechnics and Other Colleges (1966), laid down that: 'As
mixed communities of full-time and part-time teachers and students, they will
as a whole have closer and more direct links with industry, business and the
professions.' Reference was made to the fact that 'The Secretary of State is also
anxious that mutually advantageous links with universities shall be developed
through sharing of staff, joint use of communal and other facilities and in other
ways.' However, there has been little response, and not least because of the
difficulties of co-operation across the binary line.

The binary line was substantially strengthened in 1981 through the creation of the NAB, and the factors conducive to a relatively, closed-system view of the universities were, thereby, accentuated. It appears that the universities and the UGC were, generally speaking, content to see the increasingly competitive, non-autonomous sector of higher education tidied up financially and brought within a tighter and more constraining framework of control. Both the traditional academic ethic and the tendencies towards undue academicism within the universities were effectively given additional protection in terms of national policy. Others, on the less favoured side of the binary line, were expected to deal with the continuing demand for student places and with many of the needs of industry, commerce, the professions and the public services. However, the strategic sense of the UGC and the CVCP had failed to detect two potentially damaging precedents for their own sector: the awkward comparison of increasingly divergent unit costs for undergraduate education; and a sharp increase in the potential for politicization both within the control system and within institutions. The NAB itself was at best a political device to appease the local authority associations by giving them essentially a position of veto and control within the superior Committee. It was a political device also in the sense that the lower Board – preferred initially as the 'power house' of the NAB – was weakened further by being made up for the most part of the representatives of competing interests. The weakness of the position of the Chairman of the Board in the face of the controlling position of the Committee and its zealous protection of local authority interests, was to prove as disastrous as it was predictable. It is clear that a major outcome of the creation of the NAB has been to demonstrate how politicized a control system in higher education can become if the co-ordinated strength of leadership within the institutions is not brought to bear successfully on policy-making by government – the CDP and the CVCP failed to achieve this. It is no accident that this period has seen also a marked increase in politicization at the institutional level, particularly within the non-autonomous sector, with examples of the undermining of the detachment of governing bodies in working with their directors and academic boards, through alliances between local authority members and political activists among staff and student members. Such actions inevitably weaken autonomy, institutional coherence and the capacity to plan and act effectively.

The present government proposals to bring the polytechnics (and other major colleges) under central control evidently takes account of the severe deficiencies of the local authority system as it relates to higher education, including the long-standing need on grounds of efficiency alone for the polytechnics, at least, to be given the corporate status and, therefore, the operating autonomy essential to large and vigorous institutions. However, it is by no means clear that the binary divide will be softened in the process. If it is not, the universities will continue to be protected within a framework of values and objectives which is insufficiently attuned to the needs of both scholarship and society, whilst the polytechnics with their strongly operational concerns will continue to receive less than an appropriate share of resources and recognition. The government could have taken more serious note of the advice of the Parliamentary Select Committee on Education, Sciences and the Arts (1979–80) to review after five years the relationship between the NAB and the UGC. It could also have responded to the recommendation from the *Leverhulme Programme of Study into the Future of Higher Education* (1983) that an overarching, advisory body should be created. It has become clear that a strategic planning body for the whole of higher education is essential. Such a body would need to undertake a reappraisal of the roles which need to be discharged by institutions of higher education and the way in which they could be inter-related at the system level.

The current period of financial retrenchment in higher education and its associated external pressures to examine performance and accountability, has of course brought some positive responses from all parts of higher education. However, defensive rather than constructive responses have been all too evident. Such responses have contributed further to the weakening of the public standing of higher education, and have enabled the resolute pragmatism of government in enforcing change to proceed without sufficient questioning. A searching and principled response by higher education itself which deals with the basic requirements of scholarship and with the pressing needs of society, and so puts higher education in a position of leadership, is still awaited. Ashby (1974) sensed the importance of a more self-reliant, collective policy stance in higher education: 'What is needed is a collective autonomy of *independent* corporations, each of which retains freedom for diversity but which together present a common front on matters of vital importance.'

The difficulties, hitherto, in achieving this desirable state of affairs can be seen with chastening hindsight in the generally 'dusty' response given to Shirley Williams, as Secretary of State, when she circulated in 1969 her 'Thirteen Points' for consideration within the universities. The thirteen points bore directly on the capacity and the willingness of the university system to operate more economically and also to increase the number of places available for students. I recall now with some discomfort, as others must, the negative and even disdainful reaction of my own university at the time, Leeds – a university not traditionally retreatist and one led at the time by a Vice-Chancellor from the world of affairs. This rather short-sighted reaction is evident from the published letter addressed by the CVCP to the Vice-Chancellors (1969), in which the primary concern appears to be to hold the line and to encourage a search for a solution, at least to the problem of student numbers, among the emerging polytechnics and colleges.

Generally speaking, the universities have been astonishingly slow (perhaps because of their overly internalized perspective) to accept that financial re-trenchment is not only about reducing costs but also about accountability as a publicly-financed service. The fact that the establishment of the Jarratt Com-mittee, to report on *Efficiency Studies in Universities* (1985), came so late, and had to rest substantially on the initiative of the Secretary of State, is witness to this blinkered view. Likewise, the often reactionary university responses to Jarratt and to the notion that greater efficiency need not imply a cramping of individual or institutional creativity nor a loss of basic academic freedoms, have underlined the continuing difficulties. Institutional leaders will need to bring their, perhaps overly-sheltered, colleagues to face these issues more directly and responsibly, not only as research workers and teachers but as citizens. It is not unreasonable for the public and for government, faced with serious problems of change and adjustment, to look to higher education, with its reservoir of able and trained minds, for initiative and flexibility in dealing with its own problems, and for a lead wherever possible in dealing with those of society. In the absence of convincing responses, higher education is likely to continue to be exposed to more intrusive actions on the part of government than is either necessary or desirable.

Reviewing, albeit partially, the emergence and persistence within British higher education of tendencies towards a relatively closed-system view of its responsibilities points to some important conclusions, but also requires some additional observations:

1   The rich and valuable traditions of the liberal university have survived and adjusted to the scholastic pressures of the concept of the research university. This survival is perhaps above all a tribute to the influence on higher education as a whole of the Oxbridge collegiate and tutorial approach to learning – an approach which has placed emphasis on socialization within the intellectual élite of the country as well as the development of the mind. The collegiate system itself has been a physical and a social manifestation of the relatively closed view of university life – and it is of interest that the UGC has placed considerable emphasis on the provision of collegiate or surrogate collegiate forms of accommodation and social provision within the civic universities and the newer universities. It is also of interest that such provision has not in general been considered necessary in the development of the polytechnics – the presumption being presumably that students in the more 'earthy', operational fields of study, bearing on the technologies and the newer learned professions, do not require the same level of socialization nor the same liberal intellects; they are perhaps judged to be nearer to the world of 'trade' and need not be so civilized!

2   The aspect of the liberal university which is associated with a general education (in the sense of being broad and liberalizing) has not been preserved to any great extent outside Oxbridge and perhaps some of the newer universities. It has succumbed to another of the distinctive features of the traditional university, namely, the discipline-based education of the student in the context of research. In the United States the implied conflict of interest was resolved differently – the undergraduate college, with a 'liberal arts' programme, was preserved alongside the graduate school in which the concept of the research university could receive full expression, and alongside the professional school within which the operational needs of research and learning could be pursued. The British solution, outside to some extent 'Oxbridge' and some of the newer universities, has been to force the pattern of undergraduate study into the disciplinary structure of the research university and to assert that a general education (in the sense of acquiring general qualities of the mind) could be achieved by study in depth under the tutorship of research scholars with narrowly specialized concerns. The research context of such education is determined by the perceptions of

specialist peer groups, Halsey's (1971) 'invisible colleges', without serious reference to the world outside and its essentially interdisciplinary problems – the world in which most graduates will utilize their knowledge and intellectual skills. As Milward and Studdert-Kennedy (1984) observed:

> The university teacher judges his expertise and receives his rewards for the most part within the framework of one subject. His courses and examinations belong to the traditions of that subject, his publications are judged by other teachers in that subject, he attends its annual conferences and, if successful, is promoted through a small and fairly familiar peer group to a chair from which he continues to organize the teaching of the same subject. There are great penalties in breaking out of this cocoon into an insecure world of fewer peers, fewer conferences, and fewer senior posts; and the best and most confident of teachers is quite justified in looking very hard at what sort of prospects the system offers him if he once casts aside his subject label.

3   Basic research within the academic disciplines is concerned, in principle, with the search for universal truths and values – abstraction and generality are therefore at a premium. This has two important consequences. First, the relationship between theory and action is not necessarily a serious concern and may indeed be seen as an unnecessary diversion. Second, the under-graduate is expected to model his intellectual development on that of his researcher mentor with a consequent bias towards the success of those students who enjoy dealing with abstractions. Yet it is entirely clear that there are many able students who derive their strongest motivation for serious intellectual enquiry when the problems at issue have to be related directly to the world of affairs as well as to that of scholarship.

4   In a relatively closed academic system, within which the drive is towards the progressive validation of the basic disciplines through research and teaching, there is a disposition to mark down and even malign more operational fields of research and teaching, particularly if they are related directly to a career. Scott (1984) has commented on the extremes of what he calls 'academicism' and its divisive effects within scholarship and between scholarship and the extrinsic world of affairs.

5   It is inevitable that institutions of higher education distinguished by a high degree of academicism should find it difficult, or indeed an unnecessary intrusion upon their central concerns, to interact closely with industry, commerce and the professions. However, it is perhaps a matter of some surprise that the civic universities in Britain, created through the initiative and support of leaders of industry, have not found it appropriate to work more seriously at their local connections and to reflect this in their general ethos. The values which relate to a drift away from these local connections have also had a marked influence on governance in the civic universities, and in those founded later. The lay Courts and largely lay Councils have become relatively unimportant in policy matters. The essential authority has passed to the academics in the Senate, with Council taking up a largely responsive role, except in general financial matters. Moodie (1974) notes that:

By 1970, the jurisdiction of Senate had been extended, in varying degree but with formal public approval, to the fields of academic and senior non-academic appointments, of general and not merely academic legislation, and of finance. Simultaneously there had been some weakening of the litany of Council powers, where it remained at all.

A refreshingly perceptive observation on this subject has been made by Morrell (1986):

> . . . the cosy academic communities of some of the newer universities which carefuly marshalled most of the power in the hands of the Senate and treated the governing councils with courteous contempt, are now having cause to regret that conceit. There is now no doubt that the involvement of distinguished and highly-reputed laymen in the government of a university is not only one of the greatest safeguards of autonomy, but is also one of the most effective ways of communicating the ethos, purpose and benefit of the university to the surrounding community.

6   Attitudes to student admission are intimately associated with the degree to which institutions are orientated to basic disciplinary concerns and are therefore highly sensitive to conventional academic qualifications. Halsey and Trow (1971) note that:

> There can be little question that the overall quality of university students rose during the decade preceding Robbins. [However] . . . when the overwhelming majority of teachers refuse to recognize an improvement in their students during these years, while a fifth claimed that the quality of their students was deteriorating, it seems likely that these judgements are strongly influenced by the widespread fear of expansion among university teachers . . . This widespread fear of growth (or indeed of any kind of change) is a pervasive characteristic of the British academic, as of his institution.

It is necessary to conclude this chapter by underlining the fact that a critique of the tendencies for higher education to operate as a relatively closed system should not be judged as implying that the basic detachment of academics, their freedom to pursue disinterested enquiries, to publish their conclusions and to educate their students within an atmosphere of free and open enquiry, should itself be challenged. This is not at issue. The question is how best to preserve the essential autonomy of higher education given that it is a public service and must,therefore, reckon with the expectations of it, both from the public and from governments. It will be argued that a more open and interactive stance within the world of affairs is capable of reinforcing the autonomy of higher education as well as enriching its research and teaching, by demonstrating the strength and value of its contribution. It will also be argued that a realization of the sense of values and purpose which such interaction implies would require a serious reappraisal of the traditional academic ethic and its meaning in terms of research and learning.

2

Higher Education as a Public Service

It has been argued that the tendencies for a relatively closed-system mode of operation to obtain in higher education, and particularly within the universities, are a consequence of a traditional set of assumptions about the nature and responsibilities of academic institutions and about the conditions necessary for their effective discharge. Minogue (1973) captured the rationale of this traditional position in its more extreme form when he wrote: 'The remoteness of academic from practical concerns must be regarded not as a surviving tradition, but as an essential condition for the maintenance of the academic world.'

Minogue's position is flawed in two respects which bear on both principle and practice. First, serious academic enquiry into the nature of the real world and human behaviour in that world cannot proceed in isolation. Abstract modelling should take place within a real world context and be subject constantly to empirical testing including, where appropriate, testing at the practical level. Examples could be cited of the failure of unduly abstract environmental planning and economic planning models to convey the truth of real world situations, and to provide a rational basis for action. Second, in the sense that higher education in Britain has become a public service in which eighty per cent or more of the funds required are provided from the public purse, it has in principle, as well as in terms of practical politics, to concern itself with the proper expectations of society and the body politic. In other words, higher education cannot reasonably pursue issues of autonomy beyond the point at which it ceases to be publicly accountable in some important respects. As Shils (1984) observed: 'The special privileges of university autonomy are accorded in consequence of the belief of the laity that academics possess knowledge which it appreciates and desires. These privileges in turn engender obligations.'

Before discussing these obligations, in terms of broad requirements for accountability, it is important to be clear as to the necessary conditions for securing to higher education that degree of autonomy which is essential for the effective discharge of its responsibilities. The Carnegie Commission (after Embling, 1974) summarized usefully what it considered to be '. . . the most significant reasons for preserving institutional independence . . .':

A viable society requires institutions of higher education with sufficient independence so that their members feel free to comment upon, criticize, and advise on a great variety of policies and practices. Creative research and effective teaching require freedom. Great strides in higher education have been made by those institutions that were relatively free from external governmental controls. Freedom from external control facilitates intelligent planning. External control often inhibits . . . experimentation and innovation . . . Efficient operation requires that degree of institutional independence needed for intelligent management.

More specifically, eight conditions appear to bear directly on the notion of autonomy at the system and institutional levels:

1   Experience in Britain has demonstrated the value of a controlling body for the universities which is detached from government and so able to provide a substantial measure of 'protection' for institutions. Such a distancing from the political process is an important additional guarantee (in the words of Carnegie) of 'Freedom of speech, assembly and other constitutional freedoms so essential to the educational process' – freedoms which bear on the capacity of higher education to provide a detached and informed critique of society. As Bok (1984), the President of Harvard, noted in a letter to the 'Harvard Community':

> Universities have a special interest in upholding free speech. Educational institutions exist to further the search for truth and understanding and to encourage personal development. Because the right to speak freely and the opportunity to enjoy an open forum for debate are so closely related to these central purposes, the university has a stake in free speech that goes beyond that of its members. Its integrity as an institution is bound up in the maintenance of this freedom, and each denial of the right to speak diminishes the university itself in some measure.

2   The returns to investment in higher education are for the most part long-term rather than short-term. It is therefore of the utmost importance (as the Jarratt Report (1985) noted) that higher education should operate within a strategic planning framework which gives some assurance that appropriate funds will be forthcoming. The short-run and erratic financial planning characteristic of the present period of retrenchment has been particularly unfortunate in constraining that autonomy which enables institutions to plan effectively and to be innovative.

3   Effective planning and management in the allocation of resources is dependent on there being a substantial degree of flexibility within the funding made available to institutions in order to take account of the particular conditions obtaining at the time of expenditure. Given that institutions will wish to make specific bids and that governments and other funding bodies will from time to time wish to make grants to achieve specific objectives, it is

not possible for all funding to be provided within a block grant. However, the general principle of block grants is important if final decisions are to made with full information and by those close to the consequences.

4   An important underpinning of the autonomy of institutions is the right to confer their own awards: degrees, diplomas and certificates. In universities this right is covered by Royal Charter, but provision can be made without a Charter. The Council for National Academic Awards (CNAA) was created to provide through its own Charter the ability for non-university institutions to award degrees. The Council has assembled a formidable set of procedures to validate awards on the basis of peer evaluation of course documents. By so doing, the CNAA has contributed significantly to the general standard of degree courses in the non-university sector. It has, however, at times inhibited institutional expression of the particular strengths of its academic staff. It has also been very slow to recognize that the real mark of success should be to enable institutions to achieve quality through confidence and pride in their internal procedures. This need was recognized in the Lindop Report (1985) on *Academic Validation in Public Sector Higher Education*:

> We have become convinced that the best safeguard of academic standards is not external validation or any other form of external control, but the growth of the teaching institution as a self-critical academic community. Once that has happened the institution can be relied upon to establish effective internal procedures of its own for maintaining standards.

The Report went on to recommend that fully responsible institutions in these terms should become not only self-validating but should award degrees in their own right.

5   Control within the institution of the appointment and promotion of staff is rightly seen as a major feature of autonomy – one which underpins the need to ensure that appointees to the academic staff embrace the academic ethic and its particular expression in an institution. However, in the sense that these are public appointments, it is necessary that the lay bodies (Councils and Governing Bodies) should satisfy themselves that the highest standards of procedure and appraisal are followed.

6   Institutional control over the admission of individual students is, likewise, to be regarded as inseparable from autonomy, since the maintenance of standards is related (albeit not always directly) to the quality of the student intake. Control over the total number of students admitted is a more complex issue since it involves strategic and possibly political considerations relating to access and resource provision within the system as a whole. However, it is clearly essential that higher education itself should be in a position to exert considerable influence in this matter.

7   Institutional autonomy must be capable of underpinning the freedom of academic staff to determine the fields within which they are competent to research. This holds notwithstanding the need for the setting of general research priorities to embrace, at the institutional and system levels,

appropriate considerations of the public interest as well as the perceived needs of scholarship.

8   Institutions must be in a position also to decide on the disciplines and fields of study in which they are competent to offer courses of study – this freedom is inseparable from the responsibility to maintain appropriate academic standards. However, again the matter is not absolute. If institutions are to be sensitive to the views of potential employers of their students, they must clearly so arrange the design and validation of their courses as to draw upon competent external advice, whilst preserving the ultimate responsibility of decision. Reluctance by higher education to adjust course design and content to the changing needs of society as well as to advances in knowledge has raised serious questions of autonomy in a number of continental countries (notably, Germany, France, Sweden and Finland) through the institution of curriculum reform by central governments.

If the autonomy of higher education in Britain is assessed against this set of conditions, it is evident that the universities are in a favourable position, provided that the problem of longer-term financial planning can be resolved. However, the polytechnics and the colleges are much less favourably treated, having significant losses of autonomy to the NAB and the DES in terms of course approval, to the local authorities in terms particularly of financial and personnel management, and to the CNAA in terms of the validation of degree awards. Some but not all of these shortcomings will be dealt with through the proposed transfer of authority for the polytechnics and larger colleges to a Polytechnic and Colleges Funding Council (PCFC). A University Funding Council (UFC) is proposed in replacement for the UGC, with possible serious loss of authority as compared with the UGC in terms of relationships with the DES and government. On balance, it seems likely that the operating autonomy of higher education will suffer; and it is a matter of both concern and surprise that the CVCP and CDP are not (in pursuit, as it were, of Ashby's (1974) notion of 'collective autonomy') combining actively to press the case for an overall strategic planning body with the independence and the authority to safeguard the situation.

In the context of higher education as a responsible and substantially auton-omous public service, seven requirements for accountability appear to require discussion:

1   The maintenance at all levels, from the system to the individual member of staff (when acting professionally), of a non-aligned stance in public affairs is evidently a prerequisite for autonomy in relation to the political and governmental processes. This is not to say that the important task of providing a responsible critique of society and government itself should not be pursued, but it should be dealt with by reasoned argument within the limits of the professional competence of the individual person or organization.

2   Financial accountability at all levels in the system for the procedurally

correct and efficient use of public funds is an essential condition. It is important that higher education should view such accountability as flowing naturally from effective financial planning and management and the information which they generate, and not as an unnecessary, additional intrusion into these processes. The universities, in particular, have in general been resistant to this view. As Kogan (1972) noted:

> . . . one Vice-Chancellor wrote: 'I detest interference in the domestic affairs of the universities from whatever source it comes, but if I am driven to a choice between the UGC and the Comptroller and Auditor General's Department then I choose unhesitatingly the body which is largely dominated by academics.'

Financial accountability and its implications for efficient planning and management must clearly be a major and explicit concern of the lay bodies in institutions of higher education. This implies careful consideration of their relationship with the academic bodies. There would be general advantage in the Jarratt (1985) recommendation that Vice-Chancellors should chair '. . . a planning and resources committee of strictly limited size reporting to Council and Senate with . . . both academic and lay members.'

3   In a wider context, it is necessary that institutions and the system as a whole should be capable of demonstrating that achieved performance is broadly consistent with the stated objectives which were instrumental in securing allocation of public funds. This is again a matter in which the Jarratt planning and resources committees should take a particular interest. As Jarratt notes: 'Councils . . . [should] . . . assert their responsibilities in governing their institutions notably in respect of strategic plans to underpin academic decisions and structures which bring planning, resource allocation and accountability together in one corporate process . . .' This is not to suggest that a rigid relationship should exist between planning and performance – this would be intolerable and grossly inefficient in institutions which should be continuously innovative. However, it is important that the actual relationship between planned and achieved outcomes should be capable of analysis and rational explanation, both as an exercise in accountability and as a basis for well-informed forward planning.

4   Accountability in higher education in regard to the employment of staff presents the particular difficulty of the contrast in the conditions of service and day-to-day activity as between the two main groups – the academic staff and the support staff. It is therefore important to make available to the support staff, whenever possible, the opportunities of the rich environment for personal development which exists in institutions and is enjoyed as a matter of course by the academic staff. Correspondingly, it is important that, notwithstanding the relatively unscheduled lives of the academic staff, it should be evident that rigorous procedures for staff appraisal are operative. Councils in universities even more than Governing Bodies in non-university institutions have generally lost their effective role in personnel matters relating to the academic staff, as is perhaps evident from the slow

progress in instituting appraisal procedures. Yet the general personnel field is clearly one within which both the judgement and at times the specialized knowledge of lay members ought to be brought to bear.

5   Accountability in research, in the sense that it bears on considerations of quality, takes place through the 'invisible colleges' of peers both nationally and internationally. However, notwithstanding the importance of this aspect of research accountability, it must be right that informed judgements from within the world of affairs should impinge on assessments of the general significance of research and on the setting of research priorities. It is necessary, therefore, that at all levels in the system academic leaders should be appointed who are sensitive to the matter and that provision should be made for lay bodies and their members individually to be consulted.

6   There are three major dimensions to the question of educational accountability, namely, (i) access, (ii) appropriateness of courses, and (iii) quality of teaching:

   (i) General considerations of access should evidently be a matter for a body concerned with the overall planning of the system, in negotiation with government. However, in seeking to maintain educational standards and to balance this against demands for access, higher education is handicapped by the difficulty in arriving at absolutes in terms of staff–student ratios and units of resource generally. The British situation is further complicated by the fact that staff–student ratios are generally more favourable than in other countries. It is also complicated by the uneasy state of differential standards of resource provision as between the university and non-university sectors. It would appear to be very much in the interest of higher education for it to grapple with the difficult problem of defining realistic levels of resource provision for specific sets of activity, in order to seek agreement across the system as a whole and thereby to underpin both accountability and levels of resource provision. This is likely to be the only way in which educational standards can be defended and negotiations with government on general matters of access put on a more secure footing.

   (ii) Accountability to both students and potential employers for the appropriateness of courses is central to the notion of educational accountability, yet it appears to remain a major area of weakness. It is indeed remarkable that, through Robbins and in responding to Robbins, higher education has moved from a selective to a 'mass' approach to access without giving systematic consideration to the types of courses which would need to emerge. Robbins made two significant observations. First: 'The essential aim of a first degree course should be *to teach the student how to think*' (my italics). 'In so far as he is under such pressure to acquire detailed knowledge that this aim is not fulfilled, so far the course fails of its purpose.' Second, in reference to course suitability: 'By this is meant two things: that courses which concentrate on a narrow front are intrinsically unsuitable for many students who would benefit more from broader courses, and, second, that many students would be better prepared by broader courses for their future careers.' Regrettably Robbins did not ensure that these issues were acted upon.

The James Report (1972) (*Teacher Education and Training*) addressed the important question of two-year courses including their relationship to teacher education, but failed to make any serious impact. Indeed, it is a matter of some interest that after Robbins the most persuasive statement on the question of the appropriateness of undergraduate courses was made in the 1972 White Paper *Education: a Framework for Expansion:*

> The motives that impel sixth formers to seek higher education are many, various and seldom clear cut. A minority wish to continue for its own sake the study in depth of a specialized subject to the top of their bent. It is crucial for the world of scholarship, research and invention that their needs should be met. This has always been a leading function of the universities and should remain so. Some have a specific career in mind. A larger number are anxious to develop over a wide field what the Robbins Committee called the general powers of the mind, but not without questioning whether a specialized honours degree course is the best way of achieving it. Some ask for no more than a stimulating opportunity to discover where their true interests and abilities lie, others have no better reason other than involuntarily to fall in with the advice of their contemporaries. But not far from the surface of most candidates' minds is the tacit belief that higher education will go far to guarantee them a better job. All expect it to prepare them to cope more successfully with the problems that will confront them in their personal, social and working lives.
>
> It is important that the last and most widespread of these expectations should not be disappointed. The government have sympathy with the sincere desire on the part of growing numbers of students to be given more help in acquiring – and discovering how to apply – knowledge and skills related more directly to the decisions that will face them in their careers and in the world of personal and social action. This is what is meant by 'relevance'. The wider the span of student motivation the greater the need to match it with a wide and flexible choice of courses . . .

The White Paper observed with both clarity and force, and entirely reasonably, that: 'The traditions of institutional autonomy and academic freedom place squarely on the universities, polytechnics and other educational institutions responsibility for tackling these issues . . .'

It seems entirely clear that, despite the clarity and force of this statement, all too little general progress has been made. Exhortations continue. Thus, the Leverhulme enquiry (Bligh, 1982) placed emphasis on experimentation with broadly conceived but thematically-integrated two-year degree courses, followed by two years of specialization for those suitably motivated and qualified. It also stated: 'We are convinced that a more operational style of thinking (based upon problem-solving) is not incompatible with the cultivation of individual sensibility, delight and moral awareness, etc., or with the engagement at the highest level with theory.'

Three years later, in their response to the Government's Green Paper, *The Development of Higher Education into the 1990s*, the UGC and the NAB jointly argued that:

> The abilities most valued in industrial, commercial and professional life as well as in public and social administration are the transferable intellectual and personal skills. These include the ability to analyse complex issues, to identify the core of a problem and the means to solving it, to synthesise and integrate disparate elements, to clarify values, to make effective use of numerical and other information, to work cooperatively and constructively with others, and, above all perhaps, to communicate clearly both orally and in writing. A higher education system which provides its students with these skills is serving society well.

This is a splendid statement of objectives, but there is no indication as to the steps proposed to secure and to monitor a response from institutions.

Substantial changes in course design and content are of course notoriously difficult to achieve in higher education, not least because of the great investment of time and thought in what exists. However, as a serious matter of educational accountability, there is now an unacceptable gap between exhortation and action. This situation is, in many respects, the most serious part of the challenge facing higher education and will require a solution based on a purposeful reassessment of the values presupposed in undergraduate education.

(iii) The third element of educational accountability relates to the quality and standards of teaching and learning. Here it is ultimately necessary to rely on the professional responsibility and judgement of academic staff and on the effectiveness of staff appraisal procedures used by institutions. The operation of market forces also plays a part and is likely to become more important as potential students become better informed and more discriminating in their choice of courses. It would not seem appropriate to extend across all of higher education the system of Her Majesty's Inspectors which is in being in the non-university sector. Experience suggests that it is extremely difficult for inspectors to keep abreast of advances in the range of subjects which they cover and in methods of presenting these subjects. Consequently, their evaluations tend to be overly general and to bear on considerations of form rather than substance.

Accountability both for the appropriateness of courses and for the quality of teaching rests most directly with the academic boards and senates, and with institutional leaders at all levels. Traditionally, the course committees and other screening procedures established, particularly within the universities, have had a primarily reactive role – the aim in a department commonly being to get a course through such a committee rather than engage in fruitful interaction with it. It is likely that a more generally pro-active role for course committees of the type now common in the polytechnics, coupled with periodic course reviews, would be advantageous. It would not be appropriate for this work to be done by the CNAA – the report of the Lindop Committee disposed of this possibility. However, course committees in institutions could well be strengthened by external nominees approved by senates and academic boards; and it must be an important task for heads of institutions to ensure that reports of such committees are acted upon.

7   The question of social accountability, that is accountability to the wider community, both locally and nationally, for those services which flow naturally from the world of scholarship, is most appropriately discussed in Chapter 6 where the notion of a more open and interactive view of higher education is explored. However, it is necessary here to underline the central issue involved, namely, that higher education, as part of society (not a separate estate), and a part uniquely equipped to illuminate a whole range of problems within the world of affairs, should where possible take a lead in facilitating the process of change. In order to do so higher education will need to embrace within its own affairs, as well as in regard to those of society at large, the notion that change and adjustment are normal conditions.

A prerequisite for higher education coming to terms more effectively with the challenge which it faces is, then, to address more seriously the implications of its undeniable status as a public service. In so doing, it will be necessary to be clear as to the true meaning of autonomy – the essential conditions which must be preserved to underpin it and the justification for these conditions. From the strength and the privilege of a substantial measure of autonomy, it will be necessary for higher education constantly to work at the task of demonstrating that this special position is justified and honoured in practice. This will involve devising procedures of public accountability which are exemplars of good practice, not minimal responses.

3

Towards a Broader Conception of the Academic Ethic

A reconciliation of the responsibilities of higher education to scholarship and to society, within the context of its role as a public service, raises important questions for the academic ethic – considered here as the set of presuppositions about value and purpose which underpin research, teaching and learning within the generality of higher education. This is not to suggest that the fundamental basis of the academic ethic is at issue – a basis which has been effectively summarized by Shils (1984) in his essay on *The Academic Ethic*:

> It is exactly their concern that their statements, made in teaching or formulated in research, should be as true as possible, based on the most methodically gathered and analysed evidence, taking into account the state of knowledge in their own particular fields, that characterises the academic profession. That is what justifies academic life and the existence of the institutions, especially the university, which sustain that life. The more specific obligations of the academic as such, as distinct from the obligations he shares with other human beings, all flow from his concern for truths about particular things and for the idea of truth in general.

Shils's statement, however, does present difficulty as it relates to the world outside the 'private life' of the university:

> That all their work depends on this assumption is a fact which often disappears from sight when academics are immersed in their specialized research and teaching or are *distracted* [my italics] by the demands of public engagement . . . That is why it is necessary to remind university teachers of what they committed themselves to when they entered upon an academic career.

The difficulty arises from placing an unduly limited definition on the range of intellectual activities which can properly be embraced within the academic ethic – failing thereby to provide for what has been defined as an operational dimension. Shils appears to reflect such a position in arguing that: 'These other social objectives can well exist *alongside* [my italics] the methodical search for reliable knowledge in research and its communication in teaching.'

In taking up this position, Shils does not overlook what he calls the 'service' role of the university: 'There is a general consensus inside and outside the universities that they should be and are involved in the practical concerns of their societies in so far as these activities have a substantial intellectual – above all scientific – content.' However, Shils does not proceed to relate such activities to the operation of the academic ethic. Rather, he is concerned to point to the dangers in distorting academic life by the '. . . the provision of specific services in research and training . . .' and concludes in strong terms:

> It is not that all these services are useless or despicable. Some of them are outgrowths of the successes of the universities in scientific research and professional training; they are the results of the prestige won by the universities through their successes. Many of these services are valuable to society and to members of the university. Some of them bring revenue to the university which provides them. Nevertheless, they extend *the non-intellectual preoccupations of the university* [my italics] and they are distractions from the central responsibility for teaching and discovery.

It seems clear, therefore, that having recognized the problem for higher education of reconciling its responsibilities to scholarship and to society, Shils does not provide for an operational dimension within the academic ethic – one which complements basic disciplinary concerns and sets appropriate conditions for their discharge. Consequently important questions are not covered, for example: Is the real world within which research is conceived and validated to be defined in terms only of the paradigms of the basic disciplines or is it additionally to embrace the world as experienced in human affairs? And, recognizing that the vast majority of students will need to address and solve in their working lives intellectually demanding problems which involve the actual utilization and extension of their knowledge and skills, how best should a framework be provided for their effective operational as well as basic disciplinary education? I believe that an attempt must be made to answer such questions if the challenge adduced is to be met.

There are additional, derived reasons for seeking a broader definition of the academic ethic. It is, for example, important to remove, or at least soften, the tendency within the basic academic ethic to separate theory from action. This is a deep-seated problem within the high culture of Britain and finds expression in the overvaluation of abstract argument as against practical concerns. Such issues surfaced powerfully in the Finniston Report (1980) on engineering education; and the formidable conceptual as well as practical skills of such notable engineers as Brunel are well accepted. Ryle (1949) argued strongly against the presumption that theory can be separated from action – 'knowing that' from 'knowing how'. And Whitehead (1932) dealt sharply with the same general issue: 'The antithesis between a technical and a liberal education is fallacious . . . education should turn out the pupil with something he knows well and something he does well.' In other words, the academic ethic needs to give explicit recognition to an operational dimension in both research and learning in order to deal effectively with its unavoidable engagement with the world of affairs – of policy and high-level practical activity.

There is the related tendency within the narrow academic ethic to assume that intellectual excellence and rigour, and the possession of the general and high-level intellectual skills which are their mark, are capable of being achieved from learning and thinking within the basic academic disciplines. Evidently, if Whitehead's (1932) dictum that: 'Education is the acquisition of the art of the utilization of knowledge' is to be taken in its full force – if the possession of truly general and transferable intellectual skills is to imply a capacity to address significant problems within the world of affairs as well as within scholarship – it becomes essential to provide for an operational as well as a basic disciplinary dimension to the concepts of intellectual excellence and rigour. To do otherwise would be to exclude from a justifiable place within higher education a wide and growing range of high-level intellectual pursuits which underpin the older and newer learned professions and the technologies, at the levels of both research and learning. This would evidently be a nonsense.

Through broadening the conception of the academic ethic, and thereby of intellectual excellence, it should be possible to avoid more certainly some of the dangers of undue academicism in both research and learning. These include 'turning off' from intellectual pursuits many able young minds which are stimulated by the interplay between theory and action and by the sense that the hard business of thinking and learning can be directed towards the solution of significant practical as well as theoretical problems. They also include a tendency for too great an emphasis to be placed on passive rather than active learning; on memory rather than retention through true understanding and application; and on the assertion of excellence rather than its substance in the acquisition of general intellectual skills. Snyder (1971) notes how 'hidden goals' in higher education can '. . . redirect students into an "answer-oriented" versus a "problem-oriented" outlook . . . where answers become more important than the process of learning.'

In Britain, the emphasis on research and learning within the basic disciplines, which characterizes the traditional academic ethic, is emphasized by the typical structure of discipline-based departments and by the attention given to specialized, discipline-based courses of study. The educational argument is underpinned (perhaps rationalized within the traditional ethic) by the notion that such specialization permits study in depth. However, gains in analytical rigour have to be offset against losses in the lateral thinking and synthetic rigour which are essential to the acquisition of truly general intellectual skills. Rose (1986) points to the limitations of an overly-reductionist approach through the basic disciplines:

> The mode of thinking which has characterized science . . . is a reductionist one. That is, it believes not merely that to understand the world requires disassembling it into its component parts, but that these parts are in some way more fundamental than the wholes which they compose.

Argyris and Schon have both collaboratively and individually expressed similar concerns. Argyris (1982), in his book on *Reasoning, Learning and Action*, argues that the linear and reductionist procedures of much science, whilst efficient and often conclusive within the limits of the definition of the problem, derived from the theories of basic disciplines, may lead to a serious mismatch with the needs for action in the world of affairs. Schon (1983) shares the same concern, and in his influential book, *The Reflective Practitioner*, quotes from Ackoff's disavowal of the power of operations research – itself a highly reductionist and selective procedure:

> . . . managers are not confronted with problems that are independent of each other (i.e. discipline constrained) but with dynamic situations that consist of complex systems of problems that interact with each other. I shall call such situations *messes*. Problems are abstractions, extracted from messes by analysis.

Shils's central definition of the academic ethic, namely, '. . . the concern that statements made in teaching . . . or research should be as true as possible', is itself not without complication. Shils himself found it necessary, at one stage, to take up a 'relativist' (Becher and Kogan, 1980) position in regard to the notion of truth:

> There are also huge grey areas where reliable knowledge is patently not available . . . these situations impose the obligation of hard work, good judgement and self-discipline . . . Much teaching has to be done in these grey areas, *indeed many disciplines fall almost entirely within grey areas*, in teaching them to students less experienced in the subject than himself, making them aware of such uncertainties is obligatory for the teacher.

Shils does not, however, appear to reconcile this observation with his definition of the academic ethic.

The difficulty arises generally because the fact that most if not all knowledge is provisional, in the sense that statements removing all uncertainties are seldom possible, holds for both the basic disciplines and for operational fields of study and research. In operational fields, this difficulty may have additional force in the sense that such fields have at times to address problems which lie beyond the limits of a firm knowledge base or their ability to extend it. In such situations, the difficulty in forming reliable conclusions demands that special care be exercised in indicating the extent to which explanations and prescriptions for action are based on judgement as well as on basic understanding. It also demands that learning should involve some acquisition of the relevant skills in forming judgements – as is the case, for example, in the education of medical students.

In moving from the serious practical and intellectual limitations of an unduly narrow view of the academic ethic to one which is broader, and, therefore, inclusive of the significant problems which arise at the interface with the world of affairs, it is necessary to examine more fully the relationship between the basic disciplinary and the operational dimensions of research and learning. This relationship can be modelled, for a given subject, as a continuum of problems, grading from those which are essentially theoretical (and basic in this sense) at one extreme to those which are essentially practical (and operational in this sense) at the other extreme. The distribution along such a continuum of individual problems is, then, an expression both of the nature of the problems (their relative theoretical or practical significance) and of the degree of basic disciplinary and operational development of the subjects in question. Thus, in Physics, the weight of concentration of problems is at the basic, theoretical end of a continuum. By contrast, in Engineering, the distribution of problems between the two extremes is more even; that is as between engineering science and engineering technology. In Geography, with its more limited theoretical development and its close working relationship with environmental planning and management, there is again a spread of problems, but with a significant part of the theoretical drive located at the normative, operational end of a continuum rather than at the basic, empirical end. In more descriptive and interpretive disciplines, such as history, the humanities generally and parts of the social sciences, there is, by definition, not the same scope for interaction along a basic disciplinary – operational continuum. However, in respect of their theoretical orientation, the difference between these basic descriptive and interpretive disciplines and the basic theoretical disciplines is a matter of degree rather than kind (Nagel, 1961). It is important to recognize, therefore, that for the humanistic fields of study there is the possibility of their operational expression within such fields as Law, Social Work and Public Administration. That is so, in principle, if not always in practice, since there is scope for a significant flow from the humanistic disciplines of imputed theory, generalized notions of value and human behaviour, including those which relate to ethical considerations. Correspondingly, from the operational end there should be a movement of prescriptive statements, prompting analysis and response from within the basic humanist disciplines.

A broader conception of the academic ethic encompasses, therefore, both the basic, theoretical and descriptive disciplines (the scientific and humanistic subjects, together with mathematics and philosophy) and the operational fields of study (the technologies and the older and newer learned professions). They are interrelated along continua within which are distributed individual problems according to their nature and according to the relative theoretical and operational development of the subject in question. In all cases, there is implicit the flow of insights and knowledge generally between the basic and operational ends of the continua – from the basic end, validated and tentative theories and empirical knowledge; and from the operational end, normative and more rudimentary tacit theories of action, prescriptive statements and knowledge based on codified experience.

The operational dimension of higher education found early expression in the concern of the mediaeval universities with the pursuit of knowledge and its utilization within the professions of law, medicine and the Church. It gathered great strength from the technologically-induced increases in the complexity of the industrial and socio-economic fabrics and the related increases in the range and difficulty of the problems requiring solution, within both the older and the newer learned professions. It also developed in response to the emergence of the social sciences. The operational dimension is, therefore, an expression of the fact that many important problems in human affairs require the attention of purpose-trained minds with high-level and general intellectual skills. It functions most effectively within a relatively open system of values, ideas and information flows, within which interaction between scholars and society at large is encouraged and assisted by a multiplicity of formal and informal networks. Operational research and learning are, however, in no sense discrete from the basic academic disciplines – they draw upon and contribute to these disciplines and employ the same general intellectual skills. Consequently, in establishing their position intellectually within higher education, operational fields have needed to demonstrate their generality by raising their level of abstraction above that of the particular problems with which they are concerned. Correspondingly, they have needed to develop their own operational principles and theories in interaction with the theoretical knowledge of cognate basic disciplines. As Volpe (1981) observes, in the context of teacher education, but with a more general message, '. . . only the purposive interplay of conceptual schemes and practical experience can bring about the transformation necessary to enhance the adaptive potential of both the professional and his or her profession.' Some shortcomings in achieving this intellectual level and the general skills required have contributed to the notion (in principle a false one) that studies in operational fields are of lesser standing and rigour than those in the basic academic disciplines. The notion is false because the intellectual skills required and the standards to be met in dealing with the often complex problems in operational fields are of the same general kind as those required in dealing with problems from within the basic academic disciplines – the conceptual demands may often be greater.

Additional criticism of the operational dimension of learning has arisen from the fact that it is necessarily problem-centred. Simplistic critics tend to conclude that this implies a narrow, instrumental concern with knowledge – a pursuit of ends rather than the means to a stimulating and penetrating education. Such critics overlook the important conceptual disciplines of problem recognition and formulation in all academic pursuits and their relationship to the development of truly general intellectual skills. Their particular importance in the operational dimension of scholarship (and in the learned professions and technologies which characterize this dimension), arises from the fact that interrelated sets of problems provide the conceptual frameworks within which the cross-disciplinary knowledge bases and operational theory are integrated. Operational fields of study, such as medicine and management are, therefore, capable of providing the greater disciplinary breadth that Robbins argued for (and which is very much the concern of employers) as well as the focus and integration through problem-centred thinking that is often lacking in general degree courses.

A broader view of the academic ethic which embraces the basic academic and operational dimensions of research and learning, and gives them an additional sharpness and rigour through a greater use of explicitly problem-based approaches, is not of course new. It is rather a restatement of the pragmatic educational philosophy of Dewey and others. Scheffler (1965) has summarized this philosophy helpfully:

> The mind is conceived of . . . as [providing] a capacity for active generation of ideas whose function it is to solve the problems posed to an organism by its environment. The ideal education is thus one that connects general ideas with real problems and that stresses their practical bearings. It encourages imaginative theorizing but at the same insists upon the control of such theorizing by the outcome of active experimentation.

In his *Democracy and Education* (1916) Dewey wrote in criticism of a narrow and piecemeal view of academic activity:

> The counterpart of the isolation of mind from activities dealing with objects to accomplish ends is isolation from subject matter to be learned. In the traditional scheme of education, subject matter means so much material to be studied. Various branches of study represent so many independent branches each having its principles of arrangement complete within itself.

Argyris (1976 and 1982) and Schon (1971 and 1983) have followed the Dewey tradition in search of a more satisfactory relationship between theory and practice in addressing significant problems and in increasing professional effectiveness. Schon's book, *The Reflective Practitioner*, is a notable essay in the operational domain. It develops the notion of the active learner and experimenter capable, through a process of 'reflection in action', of recognizing and grasping new problem situations and so advancing both general understanding and professional performance.

The implications for research and research policy of a broader academic ethic are considerable. In particular, relatively greater attention is focused on research and related activities in fields other than the basic disciplines. This is in no sense to diminish the importance of the basic research disciplines – indeed arguments will be advanced for strengthening them. It is, rather, to seek a more realistic view of the necessary range of research activities within a higher education which reconciles more effectively its responsibilities to scholarship and to society, and so begins to examine its research priorities.

An important difficulty in achieving this reconciliation, within basic research itself, arises from the fact that its ultimate source of validation lies within the international realm of research concerned with the pursuit of universal knowledge. Consequently, the obligation of academic staff and institutions, within a broader academic ethic, to take seriously the claims upon their time and abilities of research problems having a more local interest and perhaps a less fundamental significance can result in serious tension within the research ethic. This must have been the case in the progression of British civic universities from their local community origins to national and international recognition. More recently, to take an interesting example from Sweden, Lane (1983) has shown, in his study of the creation and development of the University of Umeå in Norrland (the relatively undeveloped northern part of Sweden) how very strong these tensions have been. In the case of Umeå, they were accentuated by the strength of the local initiative in securing the founding of the University – seen as potentially a major stimulus to regional economic development. It was also accentuated by the existence (as is generally the case in Sweden) of a Regional Board for Higher Education with strong lay representation. Although this Board is not directly involved in setting research priorities, it is able to exert considerable influence. Nevertheless, it is also clear that Umeå, like its counterparts in northern Finland, has succeeded in dealing positively with the tensions. It has done so through making a significant contribution to both basic research and more operational research into regional and national problems, advancing its standing, thereby, among the older universities in Sweden and internationally.

Following on from the example of Umeå, it appears not unreasonable to argue that, within a public service, basic research workers should feel a responsibility to select their problems and set their priorities with a proper (but not exclusive) awareness of the opportunities and needs which exist locally and nationally. Likewise, it appears to be important that the conclusions from basic research should wherever possible be assessed against the extrinsic problems of the world of affairs, as well as the intrinsic body of knowledge of the scholarly disciplines. Evidently, the process should be a mutual one with the implication that both basic research and operational research are capable of receiving greater enrichment, through the interactions which form part of a broader academic ethic. This conclusion applies readily to the more theoretically-oriented disciplines and their operational counterparts. It does, however, present some difficulty in the more descriptive, humanistic fields. It is important, therefore, that these fields should give greater attention to problems which bear upon questions of value and practice in human behaviour at various levels of scale, in order that they might more commonly inform judgements made within the contemporary scene as well as illuminating the past. Shils (1949) wrote, in his Foreword to Weber's *Methodology of the Social Sciences*, that:

> . . . it does seem in the present state of social science in which theory and observation have tended to run apart from one another, and in which there has been a scatter of attention over a large number of unconnected, particular problems, that some serious consideration of the criteria of problem selection would be fruitful, and if this is coupled with an intensified awareness of the theoretical necessities entailed in concrete empirical investigation, the chances for a growth of knowledge about certain crucial problems would appear, in the light of our constantly improving technical resources, to be very good.

Correspondingly, Daiches (1982) has stressed by implication the importance of policy-related research in the humanities:

There can be little doubt that in the field of the humanities it is interpretation and evaluation that are most important. But it is not only interpretation and evaluation of works of art and historical movements and personalities, and so on, that we need; most of all we need new interpretations and evaluations of the functions of humanistic study as a whole; its role in society; its meaning in terms of people's lives and the values one seeks to encourage in living.

Allied to these arguments for the basic research disciplines reaching out wherever possible to select their problems and assess their conclusions within the context of the world of affairs as well as scholarship, is the argument for what has come to be called 'strategic research'. Such research is concerned with identifying problems at the interface between research and advancing technology (in the broadest sense) such that the basic issues in the way of achieving foreseeable technological advances can be identified and researched into. The OECD (1981) Report on *The Future of University Research* observed that:

> What seems to be required is a substantial investment in strategic research: that is to say, research addressed neither to the problems of immediate short-term relevance nor to the problems which derive their interest solely from scientific theory but having as a background a practical orientation. It is by the performance of such research that universities could make a significant contribution to the economy.

Blume (1982) cites biotechnology as a field of strategic research and refers to the joint report on the subject by the Advisory Council for Applied Research and Development (ACARD) (1980), the Royal Society and the Advisory Board for the Research Councils (ABRC) (1987). Strategic research relates not only to science and technology but also to the social sciences, at their wide and important interface with areas of public policy – including higher education.

Operational research, in the sense in which this term has been used, evidently has both a strategic and a more immediate significance. In the more immediate sense, it is concerned with the application and the refinement of existing knowledge in the solution of high-level, practical problems. Such research has an important place within a broader academic ethic, particularly when the problems at issue raise new questions of basic understanding or interpretation in a practical setting, and, therefore, generate interaction within relevant basic disciplines. This is not to say that higher education should decline to engage in more routine operational research if it is in demand and can be done without distorting strategic or basic research priorities or teaching programmes. Indeed there would be much to be gained in higher education from the more general and explicit emergence of research consultants, people no longer concerned, perhaps, to seek basic or strategic advances, but extremely skilled at immediately relevant, operational research. Such consultants would be capable of enriching the research interface with the world of affairs, identifying new problems for more basic research, and feeding into undergraduate projects and postgraduate research training programmes valuable operational experience.

The important and much respected role discharged by medical consultants in the teaching hospitals bears to some extent on this more general notion of consultants.

Within a broader academic ethic, the relationship between research and teaching requires additional comment. This relationship was central to the concept of the research university, a relationship which was clearly stated by Shils (1984):

> The Humboldtian idea of the unity of teaching and research remains a valid one . . . The ideal of the formation of the mind and character by research must also apply in teaching. Teaching is not merely the transmission of substantive, factual and theoretical knowledge. It must aim at conveying understanding of the fundamental truths in the subject and the methods of enquiry and testing characteristic of their subject.

The argument has, however, been increasingly questioned both because of the difficulties in combining successfully an active research career with undergraduate teaching and because of the possible distorting effect on such teaching of an undue concern with the researcher's own immediate interests. Carter (1980) observes:

> . . . liveliness in teaching, it is said, is encouraged by the activity of observing, experimenting and testing theory at the frontiers of knowledge; and, therefore, research in this sense should be a major part of the activity of all higher education institutions. I know of no proof of this argument and, from my own observation, I take the liberty to doubt it.

Durham and Oldham (1982) formed a comparable conclusion as part of the Leverhulme enquiry:

> There was a good deal of discussion at the seminar on the relationship between teaching and research. The generally accepted wisdom in the past has been that the two are intimately related. This view was challenged and most participants agreed that there was no evidence to support it. Some studies which have examined the issue have concluded that the reverse may be the case.

However, two contrary practical arguments appear to be important. First, if the academic ethic is to be broadened through strengthening the operational dimension of learning – if more students are to become competent in the utilization as well as the acquisition of knowledge – it is important that students should become active learners and enquirers through the influence and example of teachers who are themselves engaged in operational research. Second, if it be accepted that the truly general intellectual skills which have been argued for, and which are associated with, problem-based approaches to learning, are essentially those skills which are central to competence in research, then it become important to ensure that they are developed and understood in a research contxt.

Postgraduate study within the framework of a broader academic ethic would give greater weight to operational problems, and without distinctions of value other than those based on the intellectual difficulty of the research and its theoretical and practical significance. In the sense that the broader ethic places weight on the capacity both to create (or re-order) knowledge and to put it to work, substantial emphasis would be necessary on the process of research training. This training must include the development through a skilled supervisor of the capacity to identify, and to make manageable for research, significant problems and to plan and complete an appropriate programme of research and writing in the time available. An appropriate programme may well be at the PhD level, if the problem at issue lies within the basic disciplines or within the strategic and operational sphere. However, there is extremely important research training and intellectual development to be achieved across the academic-operational spectrum at the Masters and M.Phil. levels, particularly through the study of a series of related problems on a project basis and under close supervision. Discussions suggest that such a problem- or project-based research training is particularly appropriate to entry as an analyst within finance, industry, commerce and the public services.

A broadened conception of the academic ethic widens the scope of what is to be regarded as significant research. It therefore accentuates the problem of assessing and setting research priorities at the national level, and places emphasis on the need for role definition between institutions. Such definition would need to take place within an appropriate forum, which might grow jointly out of the present ACARD and the ABRC. Both bodies have expressed their concern for improving interaction and the flow of information between industry and higher education; and the ABRC (1987) has been forward looking (and inevitably controversial) in developing *A Strategy for the Science Base*.

Durham and Oldham (1982) have argued, within the Leverhulme enquiry, for a forum which would:

> . . . enable the views of the scientific community, government and industry to be brought together by a high level committee with representation from different interest groups. The recommendation is intended to help arrive at a consensus on the main priority areas where research funds should be concentrated. It should not be interpreted as being a device to plan or direct research itself. The purpose is to help pick the growth areas, not to stultify the individual researcher.

Durham and Oldham envisaged separate forums for the sciences and the social sciences. However, the interests of the scientific community and the 'consumers' of research would be served more effectively, at the strategic level, by a single planning body for research. Important research problems, both academic and operational, exist at the interface between the natural and the social sciences.

The implications of a broader academic ethic go well beyond research. They bear, for example, on teaching and learning, on the definition of institutional roles within a system of higher education and on the operation of the academic profession. These implications will be considered in subsequent chapters. Here it is necessary to underline finally the argument that, in order to achieve a more open and interactive system of higher education, one capable of reconciling more effectively its responsibilities to scholarship and society, it will be necessary to work towards a self-conscious broadening of the conception of the academic ethic. Such a conception will require the explicit recognition of an operational as well as a basic, disciplinary dimension in research, teaching and learning, and a systematic pursuit of its implications in planning and managing the system of higher education. Boyer and Hechinger (1981) have caught the essence of the general task, as seen in the United States:

> One point emerges with stark clarity from all we have said: higher learning and the nation's future are inextricably bound together. A new generation of Americans must be *educated for life in an increasingly complex world* [my italics]. The quest for new knowledge must be intensified to unravel still further the mysteries that perplex us. And, through civic education, students of all ages must be prepared to participate more effectively in our social institutions. As these three goals are vigorously pursued, the nation's colleges and universities will fulfil, in new and vital ways, their traditional roles of teaching, research and public service.

4
In Search of a More Purposive Liberal Education

The educational implications of embracing a wider conception of the academic ethic and the values which it presupposes are considerable. In particular, emphasis is necessary on clarifying the ongoing strengths of the liberal tradition in higher education and extending them to embrace the additional strengths available from a more explicit operational view – one able to give a more purposive thrust to liberal education. Dewey (1916) appears to have perceived this need when he wrote:

> We must not, however, divide the studies of the curriculum into the appreciative, those concerned with intrinsic value, and the instrumental, concerned with those which are of value or ends beyond themselves. The formation of proper standards in any subject depends upon a realization of the contribution which it makes to the immediate significance of experience, upon a direct appreciation.

Correspondingly, the Royal Society of Arts in its publication on *Education for Capability and Competence* (1987) commented on the absence of a sufficient sense of purpose:

> There is a serious imbalance in Britain today in the full process which is described by the two words, 'education' and 'training'. The idea of an educated person is that of a scholarly individual who has been neither educated nor trained to exercise useful skills; who is able to understand but not to act.

Peters (1973) draws upon Dewey and in so doing reinforces the argument substantially:

> Does not Dewey's educational method, which requires that learning should always be harnessed to spontaneous interest and curiosity, seem appropriate because so many people emerge from school and university with some degree of sophistication and capacity for rational reflection but with a singular lack of enthusiasm either for further theoretical pursuits or for practical activities that make frequent and open-ended demands on

their understanding? Could not his methods be seen as an attempt to close the gap between the two types of value?

Finally, O'Toole (1977), writing on *Work, Learning and the American Future*, expressed himself more forcibly:

> It is my personal conviction . . . that the purpose of higher education should be to prepare people to work in the emerging, systemic problems that beset society. At all levels of private and public institutions, there is a growing need for people capable of divergent and holistic thinking about alternative solutions to problems of the future . . . Traditional vocational and liberal approaches to higher education are inappropriate to this challenge because they are based on outmoded assumptions about the tasks that need to be done in the world . . . the discipline-based pedantic system closes minds to the new and untried, while focussing attention solely on the safe solutions of the past.

The liberal educational tradition, in both its British and American forms, has its source in the pure academic approach to higher education, and, therefore, places emphasis on learning and intellectual development through the medium of the basic disciplines. Hirst (1965) in his essay on 'Liberal Education and the Nature of Knowledge', examines the basis of this position and provides a definition of what he regards as the two essential categories of knowledge:

I   Distinct disciplines or forms of knowledge (subdivisible): mathematics, physical sciences, human sciences, history, religion, literature and the fine arts, philosophy.
II Fields of knowledge: theoretical, practical (these may or may not include elements of moral knowledge).

Hirst insists that: 'It is the distinct disciplines that basically contribute the range of unique ways we have of understanding experience, if to these is added the category of moral knowledge.'

Within this framework, Hirst sets out with great clarity his conception of liberal education and its relationship to basic disciplines:

> A liberal education approached directly in terms of the disciplines will thus be composed of the study of at least paradigm examples of all the various forms of knowledge. This study will be sufficiently detailed and sustained to give genuine insight so that pupils come to think in these terms, using the concepts, logic and criteria accurately in the different domains. It will then include generalization of the particular examples used so as to show the range of understanding in the various forms. It will also include some indication of the relations between the forms where these overlap and their significance in the major fields of knowledge, particularly the practical fields that have developed.

Hirst continues, in what appears to be rather an academically self-conscious way, to deal with his fields of knowledge:

Though a liberal education is most usually approached directly in the study of the various branches of the disciplines, I see no reason to think that this must necessarily be so. It is surely possible to construct programmes that are in the first place organized around certain fields of knowledge either theoretical or practical. The study of aspects of power, natural as well as social and political, might for instance be one element in such a scheme . . . Yet it is difficult to see how this kind of approach can be fully adequate if it does not in the end lead to a certain amount of study of the distinct disciplines themselves. For whatever ground may have been covered indirectly, a satisfactory understanding of the characteristically distinct approaches of the different forms is hardly possible without some direct gathering together of the elements of the disciplines that have been implicit in all that has been done.

In pursuit of a liberal education, Hirst is quite clear that there should be an explicit concern for the basic forms of knowledge and, in particular, for the 'distinct disciplines' – an exposure to their distinctive (indeed, for Hirst, unique) conceptual and logical structures. However, Hirst does not explain how the student is expected to achieve the comparative, cross-disciplinary understanding and integration essential to a liberal education – that is to deal with the issue of generalization referred to in his own definition of liberal education. At the same time, he appears to evince a certain ambivalence as between the particular and the general roles of the basic disciplines, when he observes:

But is then the outcome of a liberal education to be simply the achievement of a set of discrete ways of understanding experience? In a very real sense yes, but in another sense not entirely. For one thing, we have as yet not begun to understand the complex interrelations of the different forms of knowledge, for they do not only have unique features but common features too, and in addition one discipline often makes extensive use of the achievements of another.

Given this position, it is inevitable that Hirst should feel somewhat uncomfortable with his fields of knowledge, and in particular their ultimate dependence on the discrete basic disciplines. However, it appears reasonable to argue that the interdisciplinary imperatives in research (arising from the fact that the frontiers of research tend to be at the interfaces between cognate basic disciplines) indicate that thematically- and problem-related fields of knowledge are capable of drawing from and contributing to the basic disciplines and providing, thereby, a major additional dimension to learning. Hirst was evidently interested in a thematic mode of organizing the disciplines into fields of knowledge, citing the example of power as an integrating theme; and it is unfortunate from the standpoint of the present argument that he did not pursue further the philosophical implications of interdisciplinarity and their meaning for liberal education. The Nuffield Report (1975) on *Interdisciplinarity*, does not carry the matter forward significantly; though it does draw attention to the interesting experiments in Liberal Studies in Science at Manchester: '. . . students are exposed to problems in both the natural and social sciences. It is hoped that, as a result, they develop a variety of intellectual skills and approaches to different types of problem they will meet in later life.'

The American liberal arts approach to undergraduate education is cross-disciplinary but not necessarily inter-disciplinary. It is therefore more general in its subject coverage than is characteristic of discipline-oriented courses in Britain. Such programmes draw, in principle, on the whole range of basic academic disciplines with a view to conveying to students, in the words of Keller (1982) '. . . the kinds of knowledge that exist in certain important areas, how such knowledge is acquired, how it is used, and what it might mean to them personally.' However, liberal arts programmes have the inherent dangers of being at once over-ambitious and lacking in coherence. Hirst (1965) in commenting on the 1946 Harvard Report, *General Education in a Free Society*, found it to be too far reaching in its objectives and weak in its grasp of the relationship between the qualities of mind it aims to cultivate and the specific disciplinary characteristics of the forms of knowledge. My own experience as a teacher in America suggests that liberal arts programmes also tend to suffer from a lack of focus and therefore from inadequate integration – problems suggestive of the need for a more thematic and desirably problem-based approach. Hawkins (1973) in his essay, 'Liberal Education, a Modest Polemic', argued for a more obviously problem-centred approach and in effect for an explicitly operational dimension.

The outstanding difficulty presented by Hirst's (1965) general position, as it relates to my own argument, is his insistence that the generality of intellectual skills is constrained within the limits of the individual basic disciplines. This conclusion denies the possibility of the existence of the general and the transferable intellectual skills, the achievement of which has been advanced as the essential basis for intellectual excellence. Hirst argues that general intellectual skills have meaning only when they are exercised against something specific – and for Hirst something specific is a basic discipline. However, at the level of common understanding, it is necessary to respond that specific intellectual objects can exist in other forms and at a higher level of abstraction than that of the discipline. They exist in the form of problems which relate to interdisciplinary themes within and between both basic disciplinary learning and research and operational learning and research – themes such as power, human communication and urbanism. At this higher level of abstraction, more general intellectual skills necessarily come into play. Indeed, as Elliott (1975) implies, it is through the exercise of such skills that we penetrate and make use of both discipline-based and operational forms of knowledge, and so achieve greater understanding as well as more powerful skills than is possible at a purely disciplinary level. Elliott goes as far as to say in responding to Hirst:

> I shall suggest that the Forms of Knowledge owe their origin, character and achievements to the nature and operation of mental powers as the most fundamental development of the mind.

And Elliott is led, thereby, effectively to invert Hirst's argument:

> There is no good reason for . . . supposing that differences between Forms generate . . . separate sets of unique mental powers. On the contrary, in an inter-subjective context, the same psychical powers generate the logical differences.

In short, general intellectual skills must be expected to vary in their form, power and generality at different levels of abstraction. In all cases they must be exercised against something specific in order to have substantive meaning. This may be a single discipline. However, it will most usefully be a significant theoretical or practical problem, or one that is both, set in an interdisciplinary framework. Such a framework contributes directly to the achievement of a liberal education. It also creates an intellectual dynamic which is greater than that which may be expected to emerge from within the constraints of the formal disciplines. This dynamic is likely to be particularly evident when a problem situation requires elaboration in terms both of the relevant basic disciplines and the relevant operational fields of study. *It is this dynamic, and its expression through a problem-based approach to learning, which is capable of imparting a purposive thrust to liberal education.* Greater concern to exploit this possibility in teaching and learning could do much to clarify and strengthen the grasp of general and transferable intellectual skills. Among such skills, the following are likely to be particularly important:

1   An ability to conceptualize (to model intellectually) through the exercise of the imagination and the process of abstraction, the form and substance of a problem of basic disciplinary or operational significance.
2   An ability to seek out and master the knowledge base requisite to opening up a problem, defining the situation in which it is set and analysing the system of relationships which give coherence to that situation.
3   An ability to translate this analysis, through a process of 'imaginative conjecture', into a set of alternative solutions to a problem and to develop and test them rigorously and, where appropriate, quantitatively.
4   An ability to evaluate and synthesize those outcomes which are verifiable as means to solving, or if necessary redefining more clearly, the starting problem, as basis for learning and, where appropriate, action.

In the liberally and purposefully educated person these intellectual skills require, as Cross (1976) noted, the support of an ability to communicate with facility both orally and in writing, and a capacity to deal with inter-personal relations at the level of the individual and the group.

It is encouraging that the UGC and the NAB (1984), in their joint statement on *Higher Education and the Needs of Society*, have spoken in comparable terms of the importance of: '. . . transferable intellectual and personal skills', albeit without pointing the way to achieving them more certainly.

A purposive education should also enable the student to achieve a position of what Goodlad (in Bligh, 1982) has called 'authoritative uncertainty' – 'the perception of what still needs to be found out in a given field based on a depth of understanding of what is already known'. This applies with some force in developing a critical approach to the basic disciplines. It is a yet more pressing issue in operational learning where the student will need, at times, to address significant problems for which the underpinning in the basic disciplines and in the operational theories of the field itself may at times be limited. Evidently, there is an important intellectual discipline in recognizing and coping with uncertainty in regard to the reliability of knowledge. A student must learn both intellectual and practical judgement in deciding on the reliability of the basis for explanation or prescription. Some grasp of such judgemental skills appears to be an important ingredient of a liberal as well as a purposive approach to learning, and one into which undergraduates are seldom initiated before being faced by the complexities and uncertainties of the world of affairs.

It is now possible to consider, in broad terms, the extent to which the three established approaches to undergraduate education meet these conditions:

1   The highly specialized, discipline-based Honours course of study has developed in Britain through a merging, albeit imperfectly, of the traditions of a liberal education and a research university – and primarily because it accorded with the values of the relatively closed academic system. It is an education based, to use Edward Boyle's much loved and succinct expression, on 'The progressive validation through research and teaching of the basic academic disciplines'. As such, it is perhaps most correctly viewed as a professional preparation for would-be scholars – in which the basic disciplinary and the operational approaches to learning effectively are merged. Specialized degree courses are capable of providing the student with a considerable conceptual and analytical thrust. Their limitation to a single discipline does, however, run counter to the requirements for a truly liberal education and to the most appropriate conditions for acquiring general and transferable intellectual skills. Hirst's (1965) reaction to the claims for specialized disciplinary study is apposite:

> It is sometimes said . . . that the study of one major science can in itself provide the elements of a liberal education – that it can lead to the development of such abilities as effective thinking, communication, the making of relevant judgements, and even, to some extent, discrimination among values. But this facile view is seen to be quite untenable if it is once understood how these abilities are defined, and how any one form of knowledge is related to them.

General intellectual skills should, however, come into focus through the application of specialized disciplinary knowledge in problem-based project work, particularly if significant issues of both theory and practice are dealt with and integrated. It is of course, not uncommon for students in specialized courses to conclude that their richest and most formative learning experience was through the preparation of an Honours dissertation – and not least when it addresses an issue of practical significance.

2   A general degree course normally implies a concern with breadth as well as depth through the study of several disciplines or fields of knowledge. Such courses provide a liberal education and a general intellectual training through exposure to the concepts and logic of a range of disciplines.

Education of this type has flourished in the United States in the form of liberal arts programmes; and for the more intellectually motivated students it is commonly followed by specialized graduate study within a basic discipline or in a professional field. In Britain, the Robbins-induced experiments with general degree courses were for the most part unsuccessful. They suffered from the difficulty of securing focus and integration. Such courses require for their success a thematic focus within which significant basic and operational problems can be identified as a basis for project work. Given this focus, within a range of related disciplines and fields, and the extension and utilization of the acquired knowledge through problem-based projects (desirably including projects of an operational form), a purposive and liberal education is certainly achievable.

3   The term specific course of study is commonly applied to one with an essentially operational objective, such as medicine or architecture or engineering: there is a specific professional purpose. Specific courses are characteristically fairly broad and interdisciplinary – the selection of a related set of basic disciplines and other fields for study being contingent on the problems which give both focus and substance to a professionally-oriented subject. The success of such operational courses in providing for a general education, as opposed to one constrained by the practical concerns of a given profession, is dependent on the level of abstraction at which the key professional problems are examined and related to the cognate basic disciplines. Ill-informed criticism of operational courses from within the traditional academic ethic has been common. Such criticism has generally overlooked their great strength in providing a problem structure which gives a purposive framework for study and a clear test of relevance for selecting out and integrating the knowledge base, derived both from basic disciplines and from generalized experience within the profession itself. Well designed and well taught courses, with an appropriate balance between lectures and problem-based project work, can be particularly successful in providing both a liberal and a purposive education, particularly when attention is given to the relevant ethical and judgemental considerations. Indeed, part of the antagonism which operationally-oriented courses have engendered, from within the traditional academic ethic, appears to arise from their very success in motivating students for active and discriminating learning. And it may be that, just as the natural sciences have had a formative influence on approaches to higher education, so, in this period of groping towards a broader and more coherent academic ethic, the essentially operational, professional and technological courses will provide a powerful alternative model.

In seeking a more purposive extension of the values of liberal education, within a broader academic ethic, it has been necessary to draw attention frequently to the rather basic and at the same time general importance of problem-based approaches to learning – ones in which the problem structure of the field and its conceptual, substantive and methodological implications are made explicit. It is possible to concede at once that, for those who have, in Bruner's (1961) words, 'an intuitive familiarity' with significant problems and how to deal with them, an explicit concern with problem formulation can be a tedious formality. However, we have perhaps relied unduly on such people to point the way, and in so doing have not always forced our students (or ourselves) to make the conceptual effort required in teaching and learning. The following section of this chapter does, therefore, deal at some length with the nature and significance of problem-based learning and with considerations which might bear on its more widespread adoption (Birch, 1986).

In the sense that problem-based learning provides a focused and structured approach, its source is in the spirit and the method of enquiry which characterize research and which support the notion that in higher education teaching is most effectively carried on in an atmosphere of research. So regarded, problem-based learning is central to the purpose and values of higher education. Its merits, as a process of guided individual discovery and learning, were, of course, recognized many years ago by Dewey (1916) with an attractive combination of realism and idealism: realism in the sense that learning with an explicit sense of purpose was seen as an important source of student motivation and satisfaction; and idealism in the sense that the solution of significant problems (significant in theoretical or practical terms) was regarded as being at the summit of intellectual achievement.

However, despite the practical and philosophical appeal of the arguments, progress in the use of problem-based learning has been slow in higher education. Bruner was led to observe, in 1967:

> It is my hunch that it is only through the exercise of problem-solving and the effort of discovery that one learns the working heuristics of discovery, and the more one has practice the more likely is one to generalize what one has learned into a style of problem-solving or enquiry that serves for any kind of task one may encounter – or almost any kind of task. I think the matter is self-evident, but what is unclear is what kind of training and teaching produces the best effects.

Bruner's observation was made at a time when the United States was already concerned with mass rather than selective entrance to higher education, and when European countries and Japan were rapidly moving in the same direction. It is perhaps surprising that this extraordinary shift in the purpose, if not in the values, of higher education was not accompanied by a more serious concern for research into the uncertainties of the kind expressed by Bruner. As recently as 1982, Glaser noted:

> . . . that despite the continuing philosophical commitment of science educators to scientific thinking, little of current practice adequately reflects this philosophy. Although there has been much work on defining objectives of science instruction that specify problem-solving criteria, instruction that fosters and assesses problem-solving ability is far from satisfactory . . . The task is to produce a changed environment for learning – an environment in which there is a new relationship between students and their subject matter – an environment where knowledge and skill

become objects of interrogation, inquiry and extrapolation. As individuals acquire knowledge, they should be empowered to think and reason.

There have been a number of impediments to progress in problem-based learning:

1   The most persistent and in many ways the most powerful impediment has been the widespread conservatism of academics in regard to innovation in teaching: their tendency to prefer a didactic to an interactive method – which is more demanding; and their concern to give priority to research out of both scholarly interest and a concern for professional advancement. In this connection, it is salutary to note the action taken by governments in a number of European countries to accelerate curriculum reform in higher education. This action underlines the importance of a self-critical approach by academics and of innovation on their own responsibility, as a means to preserving an important area of general autonomy.

2   Difficulty has also arisen from attempts to codify and teach technical problem-solving skills, irrespective to some extent of their connection with substantive issues – Hirst's specifics. Such attempts have been over-ambitious, stimulated in part by the development of general systems theory and by cybernetics. The consequence has been to claim too much for an extremely abstract approach to problem-based learning and, at the same time, to imply a superficiality of concern for basic knowledge.

3   The development of formal, mathematically-based techniques of problem-solving, through the war-time and post-war progress of operations research, led to their application in professional fields, including management studies. These applications tended perforce to be associated with narrow definitions of problem situations and overstressed the instrumental aspects of problem-solving. In their extreme influence on educational practice and research, such approaches brought a charge of providing 'technical fixes' rather than understanding and learning.

4   The association of problem-based learning with a politically radical approach to research and learning, for example, at Roskilde in Denmark and Bremen in West Germany, also appears to have had an adverse influence, in the sense that such experiments have suffered from an overconcern with the form of learning and its social message at the expense of substance in basic understanding.

Nevertheless, it is now possible to point to successful innovations in problem-based learning in a wide range of subjects and in a variety of countries. Three examples will suffice. The first is from medical education in which progress generally has been particularly noteworthy. It owes much to the example of the Medical School in McMaster University in Hamilton, Ontario, which was established with a clear intention of pursuing problem-based learning (Sibley, 1978; Barrows and Tamblyn, 1980; Neufeld and Chong, 1984). Students are selected with substantial attention to their personal qualities for a medical career and for their interest in the McMaster approach; it is not essential that their background should be in science. During a three-year programme, students are brought into immediate contact with medical problems. Eight units dealing with bio-medical problems are studied under the direction of a tutor and with the assistance of a multi-disciplinary team drawn from cognate departments. Students are expected to build up the knowledge base requisite to dealing effectively with the projects, using resource materials provided, drawing as necessary on staff advice and pursuing independent study. Elective courses are available together with an informal, 'fringe' programme of lectures and seminars. The final year is devoted to an internship. Motivation for learning is generally strong and the staff speak highly of the stimulus which they themselves derive from the approach. In the professional qualifying examinations, which are administered nationally, McMaster students score particularly highly on basic medical knowledge, notwithstanding the responsibility they have carried for self-directed learning. Staff take the view that student success arises from the depth of understanding and the actual integration of knowledge achieved through problem-based learning. Notwithstanding the substantial involvement of staff time in conducting this programme, their research reputation is strong and their per capita research income the highest among Canadian medical schools. Barrows and Tamblyn (1980) summarize the essence of the undertaking:

> Problem-based learning has two fundamental postulates. The first is that learning through problem-solving is much more effective for creating in a student's mind a body of knowledge usable in the future than is traditional memory-based learning. The second is that the physician skills most important for patients are problem-solving skills not memory skills.

The second example is taken from engineering. The Worcester Polytechnical Institute (WPI) has developed since the 1970s from a relatively conventional engineering college to a leader in problem-based engineering education, attracting very able students. It has done so as a result of detailed discussion and agreement among the staff. The conventional credit and semester systems have been dispensed with and students are limited to three courses of study in each of four terms. The assessment for the degree is based not on course examinations but on four projects: (i) a major engineering project with agreement reached on the problem between an internal supervisor and one from an outside organization within which the project is pursued – WPI maintains project officers in a number of major companies, with their financial assistance, and also has a project office in Washington, DC; (ii) a project in which the socio-economic significance of an engineering problem is investigated, again within and with the support of an outside organization; (iii) a long essay in which the ethical and more generally humane aspects of an engineering problem are explored, with outside assistance; (iv) a final comprehensive examination (modelled on American practice for PhD students) in the student's special field of engineering. This examination begins with a two-day investigation of a problem using all available facilities. It culminates in an oral examination conducted by a panel of the academic staff and relevant supervisors from outside organizations.

The third example is provided by the École Nationale d'Administration

(ENA) in Paris. It does, of course, have high academic standing and is ultimately concerned with operational values, in the sense that it deals with postgraduates who will enter the higher levels of the public service in France. The current activities of the ENA are particularly interesting because the new Director has moved the institution from an earlier concern with the study of basic disciplines as a preparation for problem-solving to an immediately problem-based approach. Contributors from government agencies are involved in lectures, seminars and project work. The necessary grasp of basic subjects is built up through working on projects and through independent study guided by tutors.

The essence of problem-based enquiry was summarized by Polanyi (1957) in his formative paper on 'Problem-solving':

> All our conceptions have heuristic powers; they are ever ready to identify novel instances of experience by modifying themselves so as to comprise them. The practice of skills likewise is inventive; by concentrating our purpose on the achievement of success we evoke ever new capacities in ourselves. A problem partakes of both these types of endeavour. It is a conception of something we are striving for. It is an intellectual desire for crossing a logical gap on the other side of which lies the unknown, fully marked out by our conception of it, though as yet never seen in itself.

This ability is evidently central to both learning and research in the sense that no useful investigation can begin until and unless a significant and manageable problem is identified. Graduate students are expected to take very seriously the preparation of a research proposal; and it is recognized that conceptually the most difficult part of the task is defining the problem. Assessments of professional papers commonly are concerned with the clarity with which the problem at issue is defined and the rigour with which a solution is argued. Popper (1969) caught the essence of the matter when he wrote:

> . . . what I really want to suggest is that science should be visualized as progressing from problems to problems – to problems of ever increasing depth . . . It is the problem which challenges us to learn, to advance our knowledge, to experiment and to observe.

It seems clear that teaching undergraduates within an atmosphere of research could and should concern itself more explicitly with identifying the problem at issue – Polanyi's logical gap – and with teaching the intellectual skills as well as the knowledge necessary to bridge that gap. This represents, I believe, the most basic and yet most obvious route to Ashby's (1974) '. . . thin clear stream of excellence', as well as to a generally purposive education.

In addition to the *in principle* arguments for problem-based learning, there are a number of essentially *practical* arguments having particular relevance to mass higher education:

1   In a more selective and more intimate approach to higher education than is now common, the assumption that the student could develop his mind

towards a grasp of its general powers by modelling himself on his professor probably had some validity. However, in mass higher education, it seems likely that a more structured, problem-based approach to learning would be capable of securing a higher threshold level of attainment, without cramping the style of the most able students or the gifted lecturers. Indeed, it appears to be capable of providing additional stimulus.

2   Problem-based learning makes explicit the responsibility of teachers to define clearly the gap in understanding which they wish to bridge and to convey the intellectual skills and the substantive knowledge requisite to bridging that gap.

3   Motivation for learning is an essential condition for success. In mass higher education, it is to be expected that a substantial proportion of students will need the motivation of dealing with the operational as well as the basic dimensions of a subject – this requires a problem-based approach in order to give focus and integration.

4   The general intellectual skills appropriate to solving significant problems are those which are needed in the world of affairs as well as that of scholarship. The concern which led a group of major British industrialists to claim that, as a basis for management, a short-service commission in one of the armed services could be at least as productive as a three-year degree course, appears to have related to a search for operational qualities of mind. Edward Heath, in reflecting on the final stage of negotiating British entry to the EEC, in a lecture at Bristol Polytechnic, recalled the vital problem-solving contribution of a young French civil servant, educated in the operational tradition of the Grand Écoles.

5   Problem-based learning requires students constantly to put their knowledge to work. It provides thereby the means to integrating knowledge around key theoretical and practical issues; in so doing it helps to ensure that a true understanding is achieved. The intellectual discipline acquired is likely to be substantially greater than that arising from less structured and less focused approaches to undergraduate study. And the development of confidence in the ability to act – to perform tasks – is crucial (Nuttgens, 1975)

6   As a structured method of enquiry, problem-based learning is well suited to developing student capacity for active and self-directed learning. This is important to their success as undergraduates. It is vital to their ability to develop further their intellectual skills and their knowledge base as career demands change. As Husén (1974) observed, perhaps a shade optimistically: 'A problem-centred approach to teaching can provide the perspective and the overview which will make a systems thinker of every citizen.'

The intellectual and practical arguments for problem-based learning, coupled with the evidence of significant educational achievements through its use, suggest a need for research into suitable learning models. Given the analogy drawn between problem-based learning and the general procedures of research and particularly research training, it is helpful to look for guidance to the well-established methods of science. However, the conception of such models must be sufficiently general and flexible to have relevance to the theoretically less-structured disciplines and fields of study – to the 'softer' systems of relationships within the humanities and social sciences and a number of related professional fields, as well as the 'harder' systems of relationships within the natural sciences, technologies and related professional fields. Checkland (1981) stresses the importance, in what he calls 'soft-systems thinking', of 'structuring a debate' with a view progressively to defining the central problem. Such an iterative approach is essentially one involving 'abstract reflection', as reviewed by Volpe (1981) in discussing the relevance of Piaget's concept to the integration of theory and practice. As a general concept, it bears directly on Schon's (1983) notion of 'reflection in action' – itself an iterative process '. . . in which the unexpected consequences of one action influence the design of the next one' (Schon, 1984). These are entirely general intellectual skills which properly find a place in the methods of science, broadly defined as systematized enquiry. In finding their place, such intellectual skills can help to ensure, in both research and learning, a flexible approach to the solution of problems – one not tied purely to a linear model of enquiry nor to a narrowly-conceived paradigm that is remote from the world of extrinsic experience and action. Learning models of the type envisaged would themselves contribute to the substance of a broader academic ethic as well as to the realization of a purposive, liberal education. The following outline steps pick up the earlier exemplification of general and transferable intellectual skills and might be expected to have relevance to models for problem-based learning:

1   *Recognition of a problem of basic academic or operational significance* – As Polanyi observed: 'To see a problem is a definite addition to knowledge.' It is certainly an addition to learning and a pre-requisite to active learning. Identifying and agreeing on the objective of the learning exercise is then the first step – as de Bono (1976) observed: 'The statement of the problem is no more than the description of your intended destination.'

2   *Formulation of the problem* – The gap in understanding is defined by the exercise of the imagination and by thinking through on an individual or group basis, until it is possible to conceptualize the bridge which is necessary between what the student knows and what he needs to know. It is necessary to work progressively and iteratively towards a manageable definition of a problem, particularly in the absence of a firm theoretical framework. However, this step is an important exercise in its own right and provides the conceptual basis for building the relevant knowledge base.

3   *Description of the problem situation* – From the initial formulation of the problem, the student moves on to abstract and so to conceptualize (in discussion and with guidance) the system of relationships which forms the problem situation – the context for the solution of the problem. The conceptual demands are thereby increased and are likely to lead to iterations or looping back to earlier stages in order further to clarify the problem. The enlarging sense of the nature and the referends of the problem make possible an increasingly self-directed as well as guided extension and deepening of the knowledge base and its integration; it so provides a structured and

focused means to exploring the cognate disciplines and fields of knowledge as well as to interacting with students and instructors.

4   *Identification of key relationships within the problem situation* – As the student's grasp of the problem situation is strengthened (with a continuing expectation of the need to loop back) a sense of the key relationships may be expected to emerge. This constitutes a developing model or conception of the intellectual bridge which is being sought. It so provides the basis for a yet more penetrating analysis of the system and a more incisive concern with the knowledge base.

5   *Identification of solutions* – A firm grasp of the key relationships within the problem situation provides the basis for hypothesizing solutions – for building bridges. The methods appropriate to formulating and testing the hypotheses and discriminating between them will vary with the nature of the field and the problem, including the balance of its concern with basic academic and operational issues. It is important, however, that the learning process be pushed to this level and that the student be expected to clarify the conditions necessary for establishing the validity, or otherwise, of the hypothesized solutions.

6   *Evaluation of solutions with reference to the problem* – A synthesis of what has been learned is made by evaluating the acceptable solution or solutions with reference to the final definition of the problem. The outcome could evidently be, at one extreme, a need to redefine the problem. At the other extreme, it could be the achievement of a valid explanation or an informed basis for action or both. In either case, the student will have exercised imagination within a defined framework and will have increased significantly his usable knowledge and his conceptual and analytical skills.

Such proposals for innovation and change within the intimate curricular life of higher education are bound to give rise to a whole range of critical comments: over-simplification of the notion of learning; undue scientism and even instrumentalism; insufficient concern with the humanities and indeed with the humane aspects of education. Such arguments are often overly defensive. More seriously, they could suggest an insufficient sensitivity on the part of some colleagues to the need for innovation and change *on their own responsibility*. As noted, there is now evidence from a number of European countries of public and governmental impatience about a lack of preparedness to be self-critical and innovative in curricular matters, with adverse consequences for autonomy and for learning. Moreover, it is certainly not possible to be complacent about the general level of student motivation for study. Research into models for problem-based learning might, therefore, meet some of the criticisms and advance the process of student learning.

It is necessary, finally, to relate the outcome of a search for a more purposive approach to liberal education to a viable course structure. Pippard (1972 and 1982) has argued for experiment with undergraduate courses having a two-year plus two-year structure. He envisages that the first two years would be devoted to a relatively general programme of study in the basic disciplines, integrated by a theme such as Urban Technology – that is, one of both basic disciplinary and operational significance. Desirably, such a programme should include a substantial project permitting a more specialized examination of a problem within the general theme. Pippard takes the view that courses of this type could provide for both breadth and penetration, and that success should receive a Pass degree. He envisages that the more able and strongly-motivated students might proceed (not necessarily in the same institution) to a further two years of more advanced study in an academic or professional field, leading to a Master's degree, following the Scottish example.

The general thrust of Pippard's argument was adopted in the final report of the Leverhulme enquiry, *Excellence in Diversity* (1983). This report envisaged that:

> . . . three layers of higher level study should be built on the basic two-year course. The first should be (one year) courses leading either to Honours degrees or to occupation-related postgraduate diplomas. After this, further one-year courses should lead to a variety of qualifications at the Master's level. They might be broadly divided into those that were academic and research based and those linked to particular occupations.

(Shades of the narrow academic ethic and the relatively closed-system view of higher education!)

The most appropriate and realistic way forward is, I believe, to build on Pippard's original proposal, ensuring in so doing that the first two years for a Pass degree provide for interdisciplinary study (that is a liberal approach) integrated by at least one major problem-based project capable of giving additional depth and desirably serious experience of operational thinking. In the final two years (for an Honours bachelor degree) a basic disciplinary and operational balance could be preserved for some students. Others would look for greater specialization in either basic disciplines or operational fields of study. In each case, subject-based and problem-based learning should be integrated. Research for postgraduate study could be built on each version of the final two years of undergraduate study; and would benefit greatly from their concern with subject-based as well as problem-based enquiry.

Realistically, it is necessary to envisage substantial pressure within higher education to persist with the relatively specialized three-year and four-year Honours degree courses, of both a basic disciplinary and operational type. However, if such courses were to be an ongoing provision, they should provide all students with a grasp of the general intellectual skills and the capacity for active enquiry which arise most naturally from problem-based learning. It would, in any case, be necessary for a strategic planning body for higher education to commission detailed enquiry into the relative merits of possible course lengths and structures, and the range of choices which could be offered within the constraints of planned student numbers and the resources likely to be available. The Pippard 2 + 2 proposal, as presented here, would emerge convincingly in both educational and resource terms. In educational terms, it has the great attribute of providing a graduated progression through a purposive approach to liberal study.

5

Some Requirements for a More Interactive and Open System of Higher Education

The conception of a broader academic ethic, which has been argued, is broadly consistent with public perceptions of the role and responsibility of higher education. It is also generally consistent with government policies and with the expectations of industry, commerce and the professions. It is not, however, immediately reconcilable with the often strongly held, traditional views in higher education which are expressed in the persistent tendencies towards a relatively closed-system mode of operation. This being so, a basic requirement for the emergence of a broader academic ethic is a greater preparedness to embrace a wider set of values and sense of purpose, and to pursue them in more effective interaction with the world of affairs. Such interaction will not come easily: it is demanding in personal terms, it is time consuming, and it is often seen as a diversion from pursuits which are judged to be intellectually and professionally more rewarding. Conviction of the benefits of achieving a more interactive relationship will, therefore, need to be built up progressively at all levels within the system of higher education. Such a process will require convinced, clear-minded and resolute leadership; and the scale and importance of the task demand that such leadership be exercised initially at the level of an overall body for the planning and management of higher education.

An essential argument, then, for an overall strategic planning body for higher education is that it would occupy a nodal and commanding position within a whole series of formal and informal networks of interaction between higher education and the world of affairs. In order to achieve its purpose, such a body would need to be independent from government, but able to bring to bear effectively on the formation of government policies the benefits of its own conclusions. Its members would, therefore, need to be distinguished and skilled in policy matters, and appointed in their own right. They would be drawn not only from higher education, but from industry, commerce, the professions and the public service. Such a body would, in its membership and its deliberations, be able to give both substance and force to the notion of interaction and to that of a broader academic ethic.

It is, therefore, unfortunate that the recent White Paper, *Higher Education: meeting the challenge* (1987), explicitly rejects the related notion of what is termed an 'overarching body', as being inappropriate at this stage – and appears to envisage the DES discharging this role. The pragmatic belief in the capacity of the DES and a reformed UGC and NAB to effect suitable strategic thinking and, above all, to achieve a significant shift in the academic ethic, seriously under-estimates the magnitude of the changes which need to be brought about. It may be that there is an implicit belief in the capacity of market forces to bring about such changes and a disposition to look at their efficacy in the United States. In the United States, however, the entrepreneurial and more openly interactive instincts within its culture have deep historical roots which have profoundly affected policy-making in higher education. Major private institutions have played a leading role. The Massachusetts Institute of Technology (MIT), for example, was founded:

> . . . to create a new kind of educational institution relevant to the times and to the nation's needs, where students would be educated in the application as well as the acquisition of knowledge. (MIT, *Bulletin*, 1984)

Leland Stanford spoke within a corresponding set of values when founding Stanford University:

> I have been impressed with the fact that of all the young men who come to me with letters of introduction from the East, the most helpless class are the college men . . . They are generally prepossessing and of good stock, but when they seek employment and I ask them what they can do, they say, 'Anything'. They have no definite purpose. It is to overcome that condition, to give an education that shall not have that result, which I hope will be the aim of this University. (Cheit, 1975)

Private initiatives were complemented by the foundation of the land grant colleges under the Morrill Act of 1862. The Act laid the basis for the emergence of major state universities charged with embracing a broad and interactive sense of their role, including close links with their local and state-wide communities. In commenting on this role, as it relates to Britain, Williams and Blackstone (1983) are very much to the point:

> Higher education institutions in Britain should have a similar concern with public service. Some of the funds they receive should be given in the expectation that they will be put to this kind of use. Academic staff of universities and other colleges should be able to claim credit for the efforts they put into appropriate participation in national and local industrial and community enterprises . . . Promotion boards should take public service into account along with teaching and research performance.

In Sweden, where a highly traditional approach to higher education had been characteristic, successive 'reforms' were undertaken by central government through the National Board of Universities and Colleges (UHA). The UHA is directed by a board of governors with a wide range of members representing public interests including higher education and chaired by an academic, who is the Chancellor. It works closely with six regional boards, which also have substantial lay representation. An impressive pattern of interaction has developed at the national and regional levels and a broader academic ethic has been achieved, within which the notion of preparing students for the world of work has a central place. Whilst this arrangement is often criticized by academics as being bureaucratic, it has not proved intrusive in terms of essential matters of institutional autonomy. And there is little doubt that the mutual understanding that has been promoted is an important factor in the high level of public esteem for higher education and the expression of this in sustained and generous support from the central government.

The Swedish example raises the important question of the regional level of interaction in higher education. A general consideration of this topic has been undertaken by the OECD (1984) in its report on *New Forms of Co-operation and Communication between Industry and the Universities*. It concludes:

> . . . one major goal of long-term policies for strengthening university-industry relations will be the creation or extension of socio-technical communities which provide opportunities for people with different back-grounds (large high-technology firms, mature industries, small firms, regional and national governments, traditional as well as new universities, scientists of all disciplines) to become personally acquainted, to understand their respective motivations, interests and constraints, and to explore the possibilities and mutual benefits offered by co-operation.

The OECD Report cites the example of the strong regional orientation of the new universities in Finland, such as Oulu and Kuopio, each of which reflects this orientation in its research and teaching programmes. Oulu, for example, has established the Research Institute for Northern Finland which receives financial support from central and local government as well as from industry. It has an influential role in relation to industry in the North as well as an active programme of basic research. Moreover, discussions indicate that it regards these activities as being mutually supportive. By contrast, within the more traditional University of Helsinki, the Centre for Research and Training, established at Lahti to the north of the capital, has had a more difficult but now successful history in building up its regional role.

In France, effective steps have been taken to stimulate the existing universities to a stronger role in the socio-economic life of the regions. This has been assisted by the creation of the Instituts Universitaires de Technologie in association with major universities. Regional Chambers of Commerce have also played a significant role. They have been aided by the general concern of the central government to strengthen its regional policies, as is exemplified by the opening of regional offices of the Centre National de la Récherche Scientifique.

In Britain, the situation is less satisfactory and appears to suffer from a lack of overall planning and direction. Thus, the regional broker scheme of the SERC does not appear to have had a substantial influence. Correspondingly, the government-sponsored, PICKUP scheme (Professional, Industrial and Commercial Updating) has been patchy in its influence. The possibilities for the latter scheme are well expressed in the Coventry Consortium, led by the

University of Warwick and involving the Lanchester-Coventry Polytechnic, local authorities, government agencies and industry. Science parks are, in principle, important constituents of regional, socio-technical communities. In the United States, there are examples of substantial success related to the influence of major universities, notably on the periphery of Boston around Highway 128 and in the Palo Alto district of California. British achievements are more limited. However, progress has been made around Cambridge; and other examples are to be found in relation to the Heriot-Watt University in Edinburgh, in association with the University of Warwick in Coventry, as a result of an initiative from Aston University in Birmingham, and in relation to Imperial College near Ascot and the M4 motorway.

At the institutional level, there is a variety of reactions to the notion of developing networks of linkages both regionally and nationally. In West Germany, discussions with the Rector of a leading university brought a restatement of the essential concept of the Humboldtian University, with its belief in pure academic research and learning. The Rector was interested to talk with industrialists, but believed that positive leadership towards a more interactive relationship might be seen by some academic staff to affront their right to research and teach with reference only to their own interests – a right embodied in the laws of the university. In West Germany, it is necessary to look to the newer universities such as Bochum and Dortmund and to the Technische Hochschulen and Fachoschulen for strongly interactive and operational concerns.

In Japan, an essentially traditional university system has not, for the most part, built up a serious pattern of interaction with industry. Individual pro-fessors have developed private arrangements with major companies. And the new University of Tskuba, to the north of Tokyo, has developed strongly in juxtaposition with leading government research establishments. However, as the ACARD (1983) Report notes:

> University research does not seem to have the same status or role as a source of innovation as is the case in the USA and Europe. Only a modest proportion of Japan's universities enjoy a reputation for high-grade research which is relevant to industrial innovation. Firms do not generally look to universities for their ideas, the larger and more important of them preferring to carry out their own basic research.

By contrast, in the United States and Canada it is common practice for universities, and often their Presidents personally, to establish consultative bodies drawn from industry, commerce and the professions, with a view to promoting mutually beneficial interaction. On this basis, major private insti-tutions, such as Stanford, have succeeded in building up large investments, particularly but not exclusively in science and technology – and without detriment to their intellectual detachment and autonomy. At Stanford, for example, a group of industrial sponsors, led by Hewlett-Packard, have made possible the establishment of a Center for Integrated Systems. The purpose of the Center is to conduct research, to train a substantial number of well-qualified graduate students and to conduct workshops and short courses for the purpose of technology transfer. The policies of the Center are a matter for a committee of the University, with which ultimate control rests.

The University of Waterloo in Ontario provides an interesting example of a publicly-financed and smaller institution which has been highly successful in establishing an interactive relationship with industry and with government research and development. The President's Advisory Council, made up of distinguished lay members from a wide variety of fields, receives regular presentations from the faculties on research and teaching programmes. The Council is thus in a position to offer advice and to give support. It is significant that this relatively new university, with some disadvantages of history and location, has been outstandingly successful in building its reputation within the basic disciplinary and operational dimensions of research and learning. As a consequence, it has achieved a leading position in Ontario in attracting highly-qualified students and research funds.

In Britain, a comparable, open and interactive approach is largely confined to the polytechnics; though in general their development in this respect is not as advanced as that of the University of Waterloo. The approach of the polytechnics is in part an expression of their original local, further education tradition of service to industry and to the wider community. It also derives, however, from a basic belief in the importance of bringing knowledge to bear in the solution of problems in the world of affairs, and of educating students in this context. Smith (1974) caught the essence of this approach in a CDP booklet, *Many Arts, Many Skills*:

> The 1966 White Paper (*A Plan for Polytechnics and Other Colleges*) rightly envisaged that closer and more direct links with industry, business and the professions would be one of the features which would distinguish the polytechnics broadly from other kinds of higher education institutions. The close and direct links are achieved, both locally and nationwide, in a number of ways – through the day-release of employees to take part-time courses, through the placement of students on sandwich courses with employing organizations for training periods of up to a year, though the provision of specially-designed short courses, through liaison on course planning, through the conduct of research projects for industry, and through industrial liaison services generally.

A number of polytechnics have been particularly successful in developing rich networks of interaction with their regional economies, notably those which enjoyed the advantage of being designated Regional Management Centres, by the DES. However, the polytechnics have not in general succeeded in associating their local universities with their work, notwithstanding the joint policy paper from the CVCP and CDP on local collaboration. An important exception is Newcastle Polytechnic which has used the medium of the economic problems of the North East to establish working links with Newcastle and Durham Universities and with Sunderland Polytechnic.

Among the universities generally, clear evidence of a concern to adopt an open and interactive style is largely confined to the former CATs, which derived their original ethos from the same source as the polytechnics. The universities of Aston, Bradford and Salford have been particularly outgoing. Yet these universities were particularly severely treated by the UGC in the 1981 retrenchment – an interesting comment on the strength of the values within the traditional academic ethic as espoused by the UGC. In many ways, the achievements of the University of Warwick in developing fruitful external links is outstanding among the universities. Like Waterloo in Ontario, Warwick has enjoyed powerful and convinced leadership in developing its pattern of interaction, locally, nationally and even internationally. In similar fashion, it has sought also successfully to establish a reputation for quality. A quotation from the Vice-Chancellor's Annual Report for 1985–86 is apposite:

> The end of the year brought the announcement by the Secretary of State for Industry . . . of the winners of the DTI's Industry Year Awards for collaboration between Universities, Polytechnics, Colleges and industry, and I am very pleased to report that the University of Warwick was the only institution to gain an award in each of the main categories: collaborative course development; collaborative training initiatives; and collaborative arrangements for the transfer of technology.

The Cranfield Institute of Technology is a special case and an impressive one, and its success is again associated with convinced and vigorous leadership. It has been adventurous and courageous in challenging the traditional notion that developing courses in consort with industry, commerce and the professions and giving corresponding emphasis to operational research, results in a distortion of values and a loss of academic standards. Cranfield's reputation is high; and it has been notably successful in building up the proportion of its income derived from non-governmental sources to over fifty per cent – so securing additional degrees of autonomy and freedom of action at the departmental as well as the institutional level.

Councils and governing bodies have an important role in projecting the ethic of institutions and in creating an attitude that is conducive to interaction. And the experience and standing of individual members can be a great asset in initiating and forging effective links. As Morrell (1986) has observed, distinguished lay members characteristically show a high degree of sensitivity to the proper detachment of the academic body and for the general autonomy of the institution.

At the level of the faculties and subject-based departments, the propensity to develop external advisory bodies and to encourage interaction generally varies with the special interests involved. However, even in departments with a strongly operational and professional orientation, such activity is by no means the norm; and in the discipline-based departments it is rare. It would clearly be beneficial, even in those departments which are thought to be relatively remote from the world of affairs, to bring together from the local and national scenes people of standing and wide experience who are competent to discuss practical matters of the relationship between research and public policy and to advise on emphases in course planning. In departments with an essentially operational role, external advisory boards are imperative.

An open and interactive institutional style can benefit greatly from the nature of the community of staff and students. In a polytechnic, with a high proportion of staff having direct industrial or professional experience, and being expected and assisted to develop these connections, an important link exists with the outside world. Likewise, in a polytechnic student body, of whom over fifty per cent are part-time and short-course students drawn from firms within the region, there is a strong natural link. In a university, the emphasis on the basic disciplines and its implications for the experience of staff necessarily produces a more inward looking attitude. Likewise, the fact that extra-mural provision for part-time students is detached from the mainstream of university life means that the possibilities of interaction with the community are reduced. Closer collaboration between neighbouring universities and polytechnics in sharing their networks and in providing part-time courses could do much to raise the general level of interaction and information transfer. Such arrangements will become all the more important as the notion of continuous professional development takes hold, and as the general concern for continuing education develops. The practical problems such as the creation of modular courses capable of being 'accessed' at various stages, in various combinations and at different places, are capable of solution – particularly with resolute leadership from a central planning body.

An important contribution to interaction between higher education and the world of work has been made by the use of sandwich-courses, particularly within the polytechnics and the former CATs. Many students are attracted by the possibility of intercalating periods of supervised placement and project work within their course of study; staff benefit from contact with outside firms and their problems; and employers place a high value on the role of such courses in inducting students to their forthcoming working lives. However, the success of sandwich-courses is necessarily related to the care with which placements are secured and students supervised. There is no doubt that in Britain a more consistently successful outcome could be achieved by following North American practice, as introduced so effectively by the Northeastern University in Boston. This practice involves a special Faculty concerned with arranging and supervising 'co-operative' placements – the very term co-operative is significant in the sense that salaried placements are made available to the university on a year-round basis. The structure of the student year is so arranged that successions of students keep the placements filled. MIT has developed its own version of the placement system in the Department of Electronic Engineering and Computer Science. For a proportion of its undergraduates, who are selected by competitive interview during their first year, placements are available in twenty high-technology firms which provide both direct experience of the research-industry interface and the possibility of employment on graduation. This particular department in MIT attracts thirty-five per cent of the current enrolment of that institution; and has shown particularly well the possibilities of interlinking research and learning in the basic disciplines and operational fields with industrial apprenticeship (Bruce, *et al.*, 1982).

Attitudes to interaction within industry, commerce, the professions and the public service are also a major consideration in relations with higher education. The evidence suggests that these attitudes are not always helpful. Thus, the ACARD (1983) Report notes that:

> Lack of appreciation of the potential value of academic contacts is consistent with the Finniston Report's view of the level of technological literacy and general education among industrialists – the UK comparing badly with Europe and Europe with Japan . . . A principal conclusion is that the initiative in forging new and productive links should lie mainly with the institutions. Industry will need to match this initiative with a constructive response and initiative of its own.

The 1984 OECD Report was also pessimistic about achievements in Britain:

> . . . the view has long been that academics and industrialists live in different worlds with little sense of each other's needs, and little of the mutual respect noted in the case of Switzerland.

The recently-established Council for Industry and Higher Education, sponsored by leading industrial concerns but involving senior academics, has the valuable purpose: '. . . to encourage industry and higher education to work together and to represent their joint thinking to government.' In a report, entitled *Towards a Partnership* (1987), the Council observes that:

> We should be glad if a high level official body, well-staffed and consistently chaired, were brought into being to consider the nation's requirements from . . . higher education . . . [and] able to take over the strategic task we hope to have initiated . . . As a matter of general principle, the education base is a public responsibility to which companies contribute through the tax system. But there is room for industry to make greater and better use of the higher education system, and for that system to exploit a paying market in industry through undertaking applied research on contract, establishing joint ventures, and meeting industry's needs for renewal and other courses for its employees. Neither is doing enough at present and the system is not organized to promote a truly successful partnership on that basis. If it were, more companies would find it natural to make a further investment in higher education (with staff time, cash or equipment) both in their own interests and as an act of social responsibility.

In a broader European context, the 1984 OECD Report on Industry–University Co-operation made the following significant comment:

> Industry . . . cannot expect to draw the full benefits offered by academic research unless it formulates its own problems and goals in terms of the

opportunities offered by contemporary science and technology. This may prove difficult for certain kinds of industries, in particular small and medium size firms, and may require assistance from outside, including especially the scientific community itself.

Individual initiatives are evidently particularly important in the development of fruitful interchanges between higher education and industry. Discussions with the Director of Research at Hewlett-Packard in Palo Alto, California, indicated that he placed great reliance on his own informal network within the research community. He was evidently disconcerted if something was published of which he was not already aware. In the same vein, the 1984 OECD Report stresses that:

> The importance of individual initiative in the formation and development of networks with industrial and academic participants cannot be overestimated. It must also be noted that these networks often begin in a regional development context.

It is, therefore, a matter of some urgency for government to recognize the magnitude of the task of securing a broader academic ethic and a more open and interactive system of higher education. Piecemeal and often unco-ordinated initiatives have not been sufficiently successful. A general approach to the problem is necessary and will require the creation of a strategic planning body for higher education. Within such a body, experienced and distinguished lay members and distinguished and broad-minded academics convinced of the need for progress, working together, would have the standing and the authority to assist in bringing about change both in higher education and in its extrinsic world.

6

Towards an Integrated System of Higher Education

In this final chapter, it is necessary to draw out some of the policy conclusions which flow from the arguments advanced and the evidence reviewed. These arguments have recognized the strengths and the successes achieved within the traditional academic ethic. However, they have also questioned its adequacy within a system of higher education which is now essentially a public service and which, as such, must address itself to the extrinsic needs of society as well as the intrinsic needs of scholarship. In order to discharge this role, higher education in Britain generally should embrace a broader conception of the academic ethic. Such a conception would carry forward the essential values of the traditional ethic. However, it would provide in addition for an explicitly operational dimension, interacting with the basic, disciplinary dimension and, therefore, within (*not* 'alongside') the academic ethic as a whole. An operational dimension is capable of enriching the basic disciplines as well as being supported by them; and it is capable of drawing these pursuits more effectively into interaction with the world of affairs, through research, consultancy and learning. Within a broader academic ethic, it would be possible to preserve and enhance the values of a liberal education by giving it a more purposive thrust. This would be achieved through developing the operational notion that knowledge should be put to work, through a more explicit concern with the general intellectual skills which are the mark of true intellectual excellence. To this end, it would be necessary to give greater attention to explicitly problem-based approaches to learning, which are the most natural vehicles for the development of truly general intellectual skills, and to do so within the specific context of problem situations. Finally, for a broader academic ethic to have serious meaning, higher education should be planned and managed as a whole, in such a way as to foster and nourish this ethic and to ensure that it is supported by a more interactive and open relationship with the world of affairs.

Bringing into effect this process of change would be complicated by the fact that currently a system of higher education, as such, does not exist. Rather, there are four relatively unco-ordinated congeries of institutions. These include, for England and Wales, the forty-five universities administered by the UGC on behalf of the DES; the thirty polytechnics and rather more than sixty colleges of higher education (CHEs) administered by the NAB on behalf of the local authorities and the DES; approximately three hundred colleges of further education (CFEs), again administered by the NAB in regard to their concern with higher education; and the small group of six institutions financed directly by the DES, including the Cranfield Institute of Technology, the Royal College of Art and the Open University.

Within the present arrangements, the most significant distinction is that between institutions controlled by the UGC and those controlled by the NAB. In practical terms, the main implication of this distinction is the separation of the two sets of major institutions, the universities and the polytechnics, by what has come to be known as the 'binary line'. Although the roles of the universities and the polytechnics are by no means discrete, they are relatively distinct. The universities are primarily concerned with providing full-time degree courses and postgraduate training in the basic academic disciplines and a smaller group of operational fields, including particularly the older learned professions of medicine and the law. The polytechnics offer both full-time and part-time courses at the diploma, degree and postgraduate levels; and are particularly concerned with operational fields of knowledge, relating especially to the newer learned professions and to the various technologies. In the polytechnics, the basic academic disciplines occupy a supporting role, albeit one which commonly finds distinctive expression for related groups of subjects. The universities have a substantially greater scale of research activity and post-graduate research training and a marked emphasis on research within the basic disciplines. In the polytechnics there is correspondingly a substantial emphasis on more operational fields of research and consultancy within outside organizations. These latter characteristics and the concern with part-time courses give the polytechnics a more active interest in the world of affairs, particularly but not exclusively in their immediate regions.

It was the stated intention of government that the polytechnics should develop not only as complementary institutions to the universities but also with 'parity of esteem' (Smith, 1974). However, parity of esteem was not attainable within a binary structure, given particularly the established standing of basic disciplinary pursuits within the high culture of Britain and the concern of the universities, and ostensibly the DES, to preserve a distinctive position for the universities. As a consequence, the polytechnics, notwithstanding the importance placed by successive governments on their role, have come to have a lower standing in the eyes of the public, including for the most part the schools and employers. This situation is compounded by the generally lower quality of buildings and amenities available to the polytechnics, the lower per student level of capital and revenue funding, and the adverse effects of local authority control on the style and efficiency of administration. The binary line has, therefore, institutionalized in a most unfortunate way the traditional value distinctions between basic disciplinary and operational pursuits in research and learning, with serious consequences for the pattern of selection of institutions by students and, therefore, for the nature of the output from higher education.

The binary line represents, even in the proposed modified form under the new Education Act, an insuperable obstacle, in both perceptual and practical terms, to the achievement of a generally broader conception of the academic ethic in British higher education. Its removal would not only provide a necessary condition for change, it would also clear the way for the creation of a unified planning and management body and, thereby, the emergence of an integrated system. An overall planning body might be called a Higher Education Council (HEC). Its purpose would be to create a framework for planning and management within which the values of a broader academic ethic were seen to prevail and within which institutions would be afforded full opportunity to express their own style and comparative advantages, through initiatives in research and learning: pluralism would thus take on a more serious meaning in an atmosphere of challenge and response rather than of dogma. This dogma, and the outmoded presuppositions concerning value and purpose in education which it represents, are deeply entrenched at all levels within the British educational system. The Leverhulme enquiry was entirely right, therefore, with reference to educational provision as a whole, to advocate the creation of an Educational Commission to concern itself with such issues generally.

In order to be fully effective an HEC would need to be concerned with both the planning and the management of higher education. It would, therefore, have a substantially wider range of responsibilities than the UGC and the NAB. These responsibilities would include defining, planning and keeping under review the division of institutional roles within an integrated system, and creating an organizational structure capable of dealing with the main groups of institution. The DES would receive (and seek) recommendations on those aspects of the planning and management of the system which had policy implications for government. These policy matters should be restricted largely to strategic considerations such as determining the overall scale of and broad priorities within expenditure on research and teaching. A restriction of this kind would be essential to an HEC being seen to have a proper independence of role and judgement, underpinned by accountability for the recommendations which it makes to government and for the decisions it makes in securing an appropriate response from the system itself.

It would be important that an HEC should adopt a consultative style of operation in relation to institutions. The purpose should be not only to create a broader academic ethic but, in association with it, an approach to planning and management capable of encouraging and not inhibiting diversity in institutional assessments of their capacities in research and teaching. Time would be necessary for thinking through and consulting on the development of such an approach – it would be important to avoid the impression of haste and expediency. An HEC would need, therefore, to be established two years in advance of its supersession of the UGC and the NAB. Likewise, some of its policies would need to be phased in over a longer period.

The Croham Report (1987), in its recommendations for a UFC, provides a valuable basis for the conception and structure of an HEC. The Report's provision for a Council of not more than fifteen members, appointed in their own right by the Secretary of State, and drawn equally from higher education and the world affairs, appears to be appropriate. Likewise, there is no need to depart from the notion of a part-time Chairman: '. . . an eminent figure with substantial experience outside the academic world combined with a strong personal interest in higher education.' The specification for a full-time Director General or chief-executive '. . . drawn from the academic world . . . and . . . of the standing and experience of successive Chairmen of the present Committee' should, however, be extended to include working experience in the world of affairs, such as research and development in industry. Four major committees would be necessary initially, each of which should include a number of Council members.

1 A Finance and Planning Committee would require strong Council representation and its membership should reflect the balance within the Council
   itself. It would need to be chaired by the Director General. The Committee
   would be responsible for preparing recommendations on the scale and
   structure of higher education, including student numbers, its broad priorities in research and teaching and its funding. To this end it would need to
   consult widely and to commission research, particularly on the general issue
   of manpower planning and the forecasting of student demand for full-time
   and part-time courses and for postgraduate training. A firm planning
   horizon of not less than three years would be necessary, with longer-range,
   indicative planning for at least six years. Sub-committees would be necessary to deal with each of the main, role-related groups of institutions, to
   receive their bids in the form of corporate, academic plans and to make
   arrangements for monitoring and reviewing periodically the implementation of such plans, at the institutional level. Given the importance of
   part-time and continuing education and the difficulties hitherto, in regard to
   resource provision and fee payments, it might well be necessary to have a
   separate Sub-Committee concerned with what will be called, following
   North American practice, Extension Divisions.
2 A Teaching Committee would carry much of the responsibility for giving
   substance to the notion of a broader academic ethic. It would comprise a
   majority (perhaps seventy-five per cent) of members from higher education
   and would need to be chaired by a Council member deeply committed to
   change towards a generally more purposive approach to liberal education.
   A number of significant policy questions would require early attention:
   (i) The length of the academic teaching year would need to be reviewed in
        relation to the needs of full-time and part-time teaching programmes
        and in relation to the more effective use of buildings and equipment. A
        case could be argued for extending the length of terms and standardiz-
        ing them, and for providing during the summer period – effectively a
        summer session – staff supervision and access to facilities for under-
        graduates and postgraduates working on projects and dissertations.
        A summer session would also provide Extension Divisions with the
        scope to run intensive course programmes.
   (ii) Further enquiry into the Pippard concept of a 2 + 2 structure for degree
        courses would show it to have great value in bringing about significant

changes in both full-time and part-time education, and in the use of the resources devoted to students. For example, an initial concern with a two-year Pass degree could embrace serious subject-based study in a related group of basic disciplines and operational fields of knowledge, focusing on an integrating theme and finding expression in problem-based project work – Pippard exemplified such a theme through Urban Technology. A major project, desirably within an operational field, could be undertaken in the summer vacation following the second year by those students not proceeding beyond the Pass degree and, there-fore, seeking employment. Provision could also be made within a two-year Pass degree for a more specific education, in which courses of the type now offered through the Business and Technician Education Council (BTEC) at the diploma level, could be amplified where necessary in their basic theoretical and operational content. Entrance qualifications for the two-year Pass degree would need to be reviewed. There might well be substantial merit in moving to a combination of examination-based qualifications (including assessed projects) and standardized assessments of aptitude and interest. Students obtaining a high standing in the Pass degree would have the opportunity to apply for a further two years of study for an Honours degree (not necessarily at the same institution), with a view either to specializing within the basic disciplines or operational subjects or to maintaining a balanced concern with both. Sandwich-placements, with a clear problem focus, would be desirable wherever appropriate; these might well be integrated with the preparation of final-year dissertations.

It would evidently be important to the success of a 2 + 2 structure of degree courses for this arrangment to be a matter of general adoption. There would inevitably be difficulties in achieving this. However, great advantages could be demonstrated to institutions generally as well as to students, and not least through enabling resources, including staff time, to be concentrated on the most able students and at an intellec-tual level which could make possible a more viable relationship between research and teaching.

There would be great advantage also in increasing through such a scheme the range of choices open to students, in terms of both full-time and part-time routes and in regard to the type and level of study to be undertaken. In order to relate a 2 + 2 structure effectively to the needs of part-time education and continuing education it would be necessary to pursue further considerations of credit transfer and modular course units.

A Teaching Committee would have a proper concern with offering advice to institutions, where necessary strong advice, on methods of teaching and learning. Research would need to be commissioned including research into the clarification of general intellectual skills and the relevance of problem-based approaches and other approaches to learning in developing such skills.

(iii) Careful consideration would need to be given to the provision of part-time courses, including arrangements for continuing education. This would require a rethinking of the role and mode of operation of university extra-mural departments along the lines of Extension Divisions in major North American universities. Extension Divisions, of the type envisaged, could be funded directly through an HEC, and could offer a wide range of services, including some on a fee-paying basis. The equivalent of a two-year, Pass degree course could be made available on a part-time basis, with provision for students obtaining an appropriate standing to move on, with grants, to a further two years of full-time study for the Honours degree. Diploma courses within the basic disciplinary-operational spectrum could be offered both as terminal qualifications and as means to enabling additional students to progress to degree courses. An active summer programme could provide courses for teachers and others able to study full-time or part-time during that period. Extension Divisions would need to buy teaching, course and staff validation and examining services from the departments within their parent universities and from other institutions within their general regions. They could also mount courses through other institutions. There would evidently be increased competition for the Open University. However, this University would retain an important and distinctive outreach role. The general field of part-time education would raise even more important financial questions than hitherto. It would be important, for example, that the per-student levels of resource provision made available to Extension Divisions through an HEC were adequate to the task. It would also be necessary that the DES should achieve progress on the vexed question of fees for part-time courses. It is likely that the most appropriate solution would be found through the adoption of a voucher system for fee payments generally in higher education, usable for either full-time or part-time study.

(iv) A Teaching Committee would need the support of 'subject' groups to give advice and to undertake specific enquiries. In an integrated system of higher education, these groups would have a broader scope than within the UGC; and the greater emphasis given to essentially operational fields of study within the professions and the technologies would itself contribute to the growth and substance of a broader academic ethic.

(v) Consideration would need to be given by a Teaching Committee, and by an HEC in offering advice to the DES, to the roles of the CNAA, BTEC and Her Majesty's Inspectorate (HMI). In the cases of both the CNAA and BTEC, it would be desirable that validation and other services should be available for purchase by institutions, but that they should be offered in competition with such services provided by the universities. It would be open to both bodies to pursue improvements in course design, teaching methods and procedures for assessment; and in these respects also to offer a fee-based consultancy service to institutions.

It is difficult to foresee a case for retaining a general Inspectorate in higher education, given the serious difficulties that inspectors face, in the context in which they work, in keeping abreast of their subjects. However, it is likely that the DES would see a continuing need for HMI in relation to teacher education.

3   A Research Committee would be a necessary part of the structure and operation of an HEC. It is envisaged that such a Committee would be constituted most appropriately as a successor body to the ABRC and ACARD, so providing a breadth of academic and well-informed lay membership, under the Chairmanship of an appropriate member of the Council of an HEC. Under such an arrangement, the present Research Councils would be responsible to the Research Committee and would be funded through the HEC. This would facilitate a rethinking of the present dual support system of funding research in the universities, and its generalization across the whole system. Research funding would, however, need to be selective both between and within institutions. It would, therefore, be an important task for the Research Committee, in consultation with the Research Councils and with institutions, to develop a strategic plan for research. Such a plan would need to emerge from within a framework embracing both basic academic and operational research; and it would need to make explicit provision for research consultancy as an integral part of the research life of appropriate institutions.

In terms of the funding of research, all institutions of university standing (to be defined) should receive a basic provision in order to nourish the relationship between research and teaching and to assist in the scholarly development of the academic staff. Beyond this, it would be necessary to limit recurrent funding for research to selected institutions, in order to ensure a sufficient concentration of resources and talent to sustain research at the highest level. Two groups of research institutions are envisaged: major research universities able to support research at an international level across a relatively broad front; and other universities capable of such a role across a more limited front only. Institutions would be invited to identify those areas of research which they believe justify funding at the highest level and to bid for support within their general academic plans. Evidently, decisions of the type envisaged made by an HEC on research funding would result in rationalization both between institutions and between subject areas. Additional funds for specific research tasks, in the form of research grants, would be available from the Research Councils in response to bids from institutions receiving the basic level of research funding. Successes and failures in the receipt of research grants, and outside research funding generally, would provide one of the bases for periodic reviews of the pattern of selective re-current funding.

4   An External Relations Committee would be necessary, at least initially. It could assist towards the achievement of a broader academic ethic through

encouraging and facilitating the development of mutually beneficial relationships between institutions and outside organizations, both locally and nationally. Such a Committee could provide an important source of information for the public and the media and could do much to project a convincing image of higher education. For the same purpose, it could arrange workshops to bring together leaders of institutions with leaders from industry, commerce, the professions and the public services. A Research Committee would be correspondingly active in improving links with research and development units in both the private and public sectors of the economy and in government.

An HEC would be responsible for funding courses of study in rather more than four hundred institutions, of which between forty and fifty might be funded for both research and teaching. In order, therefore, to make the system manageable and to distribute resources effectively, categories of institutions with defined roles would need to be recognized; and it would be important that, where appropriate, the composition of these categories should be subject to periodic review. Four categories are envisaged: (i) Major Research Universities (MRUs), (ii) Universities, (iii) Colleges of Higher Education (CHEs), and (iv) Colleges of Further Education (CFEs), in respect of their courses in higher education.

  (i) The major research and teaching universities would be capable of pursuing research at the highest level over a relatively broad spectrum of basic disciplines and operational subjects. They would offer a related range of postgraduate training courses and a 2 + 2 structure of undergraduate courses. Substantial Divisions of Extension, having faculty status, would deal with part-time courses, short courses and provide in return for fees a wide range of additional services, including course and staff validation. Staff time would be purchased from university departments and from other institutions. In order to bring together the resources and facilities appropriate to the concept of the MRU, it would be necessary to merge adjacent universities and polytechnics. Such mergers would also make possible, through sensible internal rationalization, an increased effectiveness in the deployment and utilization of resources. Mergers of the type proposed would be achieved locally, but by decision of and in consultation with an HEC. They would create universities comparable in many ways with the larger North American institutions, in the sense that they would embrace, in addition to major Extension Divisions, a wide range of faculties with essentially operational concerns, such as Technology, Business and Professional Studies and Design, and major research and postgraduate groups. Correspondingly, those faculties which give expression to basic disciplinary pursuits would be expected to strengthen their links with the operational dimension, not least in regard to student projects. The MRUs would need to develop and display a broad academic ethic and to achieve a mutually beneficial network of relationships within their regions and nationally.

  The scale and complexity of these universities and their split campuses would make necessary a strongly devolved system of planning and management, within which the faculties would assume a collegial role. Deans of Faculty would need to have an executive position and be given appropriate continuity in their appointments, perhaps on a five-year, renewable basis. A collegial approach could offset disadvantages of size by providing for smaller communities of staff and students.

It is unlikely that the resources would be available to create and sustain appropriately more than about twenty MRUs. They would include Oxford and Cambridge, the older civic universities and some of the newer universities with a civic base. Special provision would be necessary for London and for the other major conurbations of Birmingham and Manchester. Such provision appears likely to involve some mergers and the creation of overall federal systems of planning and management, following the example of the University of London. However, the essential purpose would remain, namely: to give full and powerful expression to a broader academic ethic by bringing into a more productive relationship, in research, consultancy and teaching, the basic disciplines and operational fields, by increasing the provision for mutual interaction with the world of affairs both locally and nationally, and by creating vigorous Extension Divisions capable of achieving a major regional role.

The Imperial College of Science and Technology would not fit easily into a London federation and would require special consideration. Recognizing the importance of its role and the cramped nature of its precinct, it might well be appropriate to consider a relocation. Swindon, with its existing presence of the SERC and the NERC and the prospective presence of the ESRC and the AFRC, is evidently a possibility. However alternative locations would need to be considered; and one which brought Imperial College into close interaction with Cranfield would have great advantage.

(ii) A second category of perhaps twenty *universities* would be necessary. Such universities would provide a full range of undergraduate courses, using a 2 + 2 structure, underpinned by staff research and scholarly activity generally. However, major investment in research would need to be limited to fields in which particular distinction had been achieved and could be sustained. Such universities would need to offer extension service within their urban regions; however, in general, it would not appear necessary for these to include the wider range of services, including course and staff validation, provided by the MRUs.

This category of university would be made up of the remaining universities and those polytechnics not involved in the creation of the MRUs. However, the planning of this category would involve mergers of some institutions. The general outcome would be a relatively diverse set of universities, both in terms of their distribution along a basic disciplinary-operational scale and their intensity and level of concern with research and consultancy.

(iii) The future of the sixty or more *colleges of higher education*, which have for the most part developed, within the constraints of a period of retrenchment, from an already limited base as colleges of education, would need to be assessed against forecasts of the total number of student places. Such forecasts would need to take account of additional places which might become avail-

able from within the two categories of university, arising in part from their more rational planning. It is likely that some closures and mergers of CHEs would be necessary.

In deciding on the future of this category, consideration would need to be given to the needs of teacher education: in particular, the strong arguments for teachers being trained within larger and more diverse staff and student communities, and within an urban environment of the general type in which they are most likely to work. There is evidently valuable work to be done in the CHEs at the Pass degree and diploma levels and within a spectrum of basic disciplines and operational fields, particularly when the degree is envisaged as a terminal qualification. Only exceptionally would it appear to be appropriate to offer progression to the Honours degree within a CHE, given the absence of direct financial provision for research. Extension services would be organized through the adjacent universities. Following the advice of the Lindop Report, CHEs should be in a position to apply to an HEC and the DES for recognition as degree awarding institutions under the awards regulations. This would place such institutions in a position of direct responsibility for the quality of their courses. It would be open to them, however, to buy course and staff validation services and other forms of consultancy from the CNAA, BTEC and the adjacent MRUs.

(iv) It appears to be desirable, in terms particularly of access to part-time courses, that some *colleges of further education* should retain a connection with higher education. This would reflect, in some cases, special local circumstances relating to the need for essentially specific course of study. Some provision for higher education in the CFEs, would also assist staff development and provide important part-time routes into more advanced courses in the universities. Course offerings would need to be limited to part-time and full-time diplomas and to part-time degrees, in each case both specific and general in content. In order to offer Pass degrees, CFEs would need to have a sufficient group of recognized teachers, validated by the relvant MRUs, and appropriate back-up facilities. It would assist the process of planning if arrangements were made for the CFEs to submit their proposed academic plans for higher education through the Extension Division of their chosen MRU. Such co-ordination would also assist in avoiding wasteful duplication and in providing more effective routes into the mainstream of higher education.

Institutional leadership of a higher order would be necessary in clarifying and facilitating the processes of change and adjustment which would arise from the creation of an integrated system of higher education, planned and broadly managed by an HEC. This would have its fullest meaning in regard to the MRUs. Vice-Chancellors of such universities, as in the case of the Director General of an HEC, would need to be appointed both for their scholarly standing and for their direct experience of the extrinsic world of the university. It would be important also that leadership should be followed up and supported by effective executive action. As Jarratt (1985) observed:

The tradition of vice-chancellors being scholars first and acting as Chair-men of the Senate carrying out its will, rather than leading it strongly, is changing. The shift to the style of chief executive, bearing the responsibility for leadership and effective management of the institution, is emerging and is likely to be all the more necessary in the future.

Given the importance of academic leadership in a Vice-Chancellor's role it is probable that a large proportion of appointees to such posts would continue to be senior academics from within the university system. This being so, it is important in our view that senior academics across the university system, from whom the next generation of vice-chancellors will be chosen, should be given the opportunity to improve their managerial skills through appropriate training and to gain some experience outside the university system through periods of secondment and staff exchange.

Arrangements of this type would be appropriate also in raising the quality of leadership and management at the faculty and departmental levels. It would, likewise, assist towards clarifying the role of the executive sub-systems within institutions from those concerned with policy development and consensus-seeking in committee. As Jarratt notes, an important consideration in this clarification is a clearer distinction between academic and non-academic matters – the latter commonly requiring more direct management with accountability to advisory bodies, where appropriate. Moreover, in those matters of academic policy where committee decisions involving consensus forming are important to staff motivation and commitment, there should be a clearer separation between policy-making and the judgements involved in its implementation. By according greater responsibility for exercising effective judgement to executive academic officers, subject to consultation and periodic accountability within committee, including the Senate and Council, a great deal of time could be saved – time needed for scholarly activity and teaching and for building external networks. As Handy (1977) observes, in discussing the general importance of consultative management: 'It is when the management confuses the need to be consulted with the need to participate, or feels that a minority desire to be heard means a wish to veto, that the organization of consent becomes a bog of talk and inertia.' Wagner (1982) deals with the issue specifically in the context of higher education:

> It might be possible to strike a balance between participation and effective management by moving towards a consultative mode of decision-making. Here managers would have greater discretion to take decisions, and certainly at the lower levels, committees would have an advisory and consultative function. Senates and academic boards would retain their powers over strategic decisions, but greater managerial discretion, subject to consultation, would be allowed within the strategy.

A deliberate search for a wider conception and interpretation of the academic ethic would raise important questions concerning the selection, appraisal and promotion of academic and support staff, within the context of a corporate academic plan which needed to be fulfilled. For academic staff, greater weight would need to be given, particularly in operational fields of research and teaching, to practical experience before appointment and to consultancy and secondment to outside organizations after appointment. Traditional value distinctions between research in the basic disciplines and in operational fields would need to be revised and emphasis placed on the significance of the problems addressed in both theoretical and practical terms, and on the intrinsic merits of the research itself. According additional weight to sound experiments and innovations in teaching and student assessment would also need to be an important consideration. Likewise, those staff who work hard at developing mutually beneficial links within the regional, socio-technical community should receive appropriate recognition.

Within the universities and the CHEs of an integrated system of higher education, it would be necessary to have a generalized set of salary scales and conditions of service for academic staff. However, the difficulties in attracting into higher education and retaining the most able staff (including those with industrial, professional and research experience) suggest the need for extended salary scales, above seriously-considered promotion bars. Such extended salary scales would also facilitate the recognition and rewarding of exceptional achievement generally. The scope for discretion to use such extended scales would need to differ as between the MRUs, the other universities and the CHEs.

The creation of an HEC, with responsibility for planning and managing in broad terms an integrated system of higher education, would raise worries concerning undue centralization of authority and independence from government interference, and anxieties also about institutional autonomy and individual academic freedom. Leaders at the system level would, therefore, need to take time and care in making sure and in demonstrating that such anxieties were without substance – that the strength and independence of an HEC would provide additional safeguards. Likewise, at the institutional level, leaders would need to explain and to exemplify how more effective planning and management, in a responsive and consultative mode, would be designed to promote, recognize and respond to initiatives by departments and individuals in formulating proposals and carrying them through to success. It is true that both institutions and individuals would be more accountable for their performance, and there would, therefore, be greater selectivity in formulating and approving corporate academic plans. However, this should not conceal the substantial privilege and freedom that goes with being consulted seriously on the definition of what individual and collective activities and performances might most appropriately be. Within a well planned and managed system, there is no reason for individual creativity and initiative to be cramped – indeed, in my own experience it is more likely to find fulfilment in these circumstances. More effective planning and management could also do much to remove the unnecessary uncertainties in the lives of all staff and students, and assist greatly, thereby, in building confidence and commitment.

However, given the current state of unease and low morale in higher education generally, it would clearly be sensible for any government embarking on radical change of the kind envisaged, to provide, on the basis of full and effective consultation, statutory undertakings relating to certain key issues: the independence from government of a body such as the proposed HEC, in making its recommendations and in discharging its responsibilities; the autonomy of institutions in selecting and developing sensibly and flexibly their perceived strengths, as accepted within a corporate academic plan, and in preserving their intellectual detachment and individual and collective freedoms of publication and speech, within the bounds of professional competence. In addition, an HEC could itself greatly facilitate the process of change and adjustment by arranging, through perhaps an Advisory Body on Governance and Management, for regular workshop discussions on key issues, involving its own members and officials with representatives of bodies such as the CVCP and professional staff associations.

The creation of a more open and interactive as well as an integrated system of higher education, which both embraces the full meaning of a broader academic ethic and demonstrates its efficiency and accountability, would raise confidence, and sharpen and fulfil more certainly expectations on the part of staff and students. Such a system would also be able to present a more convincing image to the public and to the world of affairs through achieving a stronger, mutual relationship between scholarship and society. As Ashby (1958) noted thirty years ago, with a strong sense of the needs of higher education as a public service devoted to the pursuit of intellectual excellence: 'The way to ensure autonomy without independence is to secure the confidence of patrons, and the way to secure this confidence is [for higher education] to show a strong sense of responsibility to society.'

References

ABRC (1987). *A Strategy for the Science Base*. London, HMSO.

ACARD, Royal Society, ABRC (1980). *Biotechnology*. Report of Joint Working Party. London, HMSO.

ACARD (1983). *Improving Research Links between Higher Education and Industry*. London, HMSO.

Argyris, C. and Schon, D. (1976). *Theory in Practice: increasing professional effectiveness*. San Francisco, Jossey-Bass.

Argyris, C. (1982). *Reasoning, Learning and Action*. San Francisco, Jossey-Bass.

Ashby, E. (1958). *Technology and the Academics*. London, Macmillan.

Ashby, E. (1971). *Any Person, Any Study*. New York, McGraw Hill.

Ashby, E. (1974). *Adapting Universities to a Technological Society*. London, Jossey-Bass.

Ashworth, J. M. (1982). Reshaping Higher Education in Britain, *Journ. Royal Soc. Arts*, Vol. CXXX. London.

Barnett, C. (1979). Education for Capability: Cantor Lecture, *Journ. Royal Soc. Arts*, Vol. CXXVII. London.

Barnett, C. (1987). The Audit of War, *The Times Higher Education Supplement*. London.

Barrows, H. S. and Tamblyn, R. M. (1980). *Problem-based Learning: an approach to medical education*. New York, Springer.

Becher, A. and Kogan, M. (1980). *Process and Structure in Higher Education*. London, Heinemann.

Birch, J. W. (1961). *The Isle of Man: a study in economic geography*. Cambridge, Cambridge University Press.

Birch, W. (1986). Towards a Model for Problem-based Learning, *Studies in Higher Education*, Vol. III, No. 1.

Bligh, D. (ed.) (1982). *Professionalism and Flexibility in Learning*, Leverhulme Programme of Study into the Future of Higher Education. Guildford, Society for Research into Higher Education.

Blume, S. S. (1982). A Framework for Analysis, in Oldham, Geoffrey (ed.), *The Future of Research*, Leverhulme Programme of Study into the Future of Higher Education, Vol. 4. Guildford, Society for Research into Higher Education.

Bok, D. (1984), in a letter to the 'Harvard Community'. Cambridge, Mass.

Boyer, E. and Hechinger, F. M. (1982). *Higher Learning in the Nation's Service*. Washington, DC, Carnegie Foundation.

Bruce, J. D. *et al.* (1982). *Lifelong Co-operative Education*. Cambridge, Mass, MIT Press.

Bruner, J. S. (1961). The Art of Discovery, *Harvard Ed. Rev.*, 31.

Bruner, J. S. (1967). *Toward a Theory of Instruction*. Cambridge, Mass., Belkuap.

Butterfield, H. (1961). *The Universities and Education Today*. London, Routledge and Kegan Paul.

Carter, C. (1980). *Higher Education for the Future*. Oxford, Blackwell.

Checkland, P. (1981). *Systems Thinking and Systems Practice*. Chichester, Wiley.

Cheit, E. F. (1975). *The Useful Arts and the Liberal Tradition*, Carnegie Commission on Higher Education. New York, McGraw Hill.

Council for Industry and Higher Education (1987). *Towards a Partnership*. London.

Croham Report (1987). *Review of the University Grants Committee*. London, HMSO.

Cross, Patricia (1976). *Accent on Learning*. New York, McGraw Hill.

Daiches, D. (1982). The Functions of Research in the Humanities, in Oldham, Geoffrey (ed.), *The Future of Research*, Leverhulme Programme of Study into the Future of Higher Education, Vol. 4. Guildford, Society for Research into Higher Education.

de Bono, E. (1976). *Teaching Thinking*. London, Smith.

Dept. of Education and Science (1966). *A Plan for Polytechnics and Colleges*. Cmd. 3006, London, HMSO.

Dept. of Education and Science (1972). *Education: a Framework for Expansion*, Cmd. 5174, London, HMSO.

Dept. of Education and Science (1985). *The Development of Higher Education into the 1990s*. Cmd. 9542, London, HMSO.

Dept. of Education and Science (1987). *Higher Education: meeting the challenge*. Cmd. 114, London, HMSO.

Dewey, J. (1916). *Democracy and Education: an Introduction to the Philosophy of Education*. New York, Macmillan.

Durham, K. and Oldham, G. (1982). Conclusions and Recommendations, in Oldham, G. (ed.), *The Future of Research*, Leverhulme Programme of Study into the Future of Higher Education, Vol. 4. Guildford, Society for Research into Higher Education.

Elliott, R. K. (1975). Education and Human Being I, in Brown, S. C. (ed.), *Philosophers Discuss Education*. London, Macmillan.

Embling, J. (1974). *A Fresh Look at Higher Education: European Implications of the Carnegie Commission Reports*. London, Elsevier.

Finniston Report (1980). *Committee of Enquiry into the Engineering Profession*. Cmd. 7794, London, HMSO.

Glaser, R. (1982). *Education and Thinking: the Role of Knowledge*, expanded version of a paper presented at the American Psychological Association.

Goodlad, S., *et al.* (1982). The Curriculum of Higher Education, in Bligh, D. (ed.), *Professionalism and Flexibility in Learning*, Leverhulme Programme of Study into the Future of Higher Education. Guildford, Society for Research into Higher Education.

Halsey, A. H. and Trow, M. (1971). *The British Academics*. London, Faber.

Handy, C. B. (1977). The Organization of Consent, in Piper, D. W. and Glatter, R. (eds), *The Changing University*. Slough, NFER.

Hawkins, D. (1973). Liberal Education: a Modest Polemic, in Kayser, C. (ed.), *Content and Context: essays in college education*. Washington, Carnegie Foundation.

Hirst, P. H. (1965). Liberal Education and the Nature of Knowledge, in Archambault, R. D. (ed.), *Philosophical Analysis and Education*. Henley, Routledge and Kegan Paul.

Husen, T. (1974). *The Learning Society*. London, Methuen.

James Report (1972). *Teacher Education and Training*. London, HMSO.

Jarratt Report (1985). *Report of the Steering Committee for Efficiency Studies in Universities*, London, CVCP.

Keller, P. (1982). *Moving the Cemetery*. Cambridge, Mass., Harvard University Press.

Kogan, M. (1972). Audit, control and freedom, in Burgess, T. (ed.), *Planning for Higher Education*. London, Cornmarket.

Lane, J.-E. (1983). *Creating the University of Norrland*. Umeå, Univ. of Umeå.

Leverhulme Programme of Study into the Future of Higher Education (1983). Vols. 1–10. Guildford, Society for Research into Higher Education.

Leverhulme Report (1983). *Excellence in Diversity*. Guildford, Society for Research into Higher Education.

Lindop Report (1985). *Academic Validation in Public Sector Higher Education*. London, HMSO.

Massachusetts Institute of Technology (1984). *Bulletin*. Cambridge, Mass.

Maxwell, N. (1984). *From Knowledge to Wisdom*. Oxford, Blackwell.

Millward, A. G. and Studdert-Kennedy, G. (1984). Crossing Subject Boundaries, *The Times Higher Educational Supplement*. London.

Minogue, K. R. (1973). *The Concept of a University*. London, Weidenfeld.

Moodie, G. (1974). *Power and Authority in British Universities*. London, Allen and Unwin.

Morrell, David W. J. (1986). Universities and their Communities, in *Beyond the Limelight*. Reading, Committee of University Administration.

Nagel, E. (1961). *The Structure of Science*. New York, McGraw Hill.

Neufeld, V. and Chong, J. P. (1984). Problem-based Professional Education in Medicine, in Goodlad, S. (ed.), *Education for the Professions: Quis Custodiet?* Guildford, Society for Research into Higher Education.

Newman, J. H. (1852). *The Idea of a University*. San Francisco, Rinehart.

Nuffield Foundation (1975). *Interdisciplinarity: a report by the group for Research and Innovation in Higher Education*. London.

Nuttgens, A. (1975). Dead hand of learning should be turned to useful skills, *The Times Higher Education Supplement*. London.

OECD (1981). *The Future of University Research*. Paris.

OECD (1984). *New Forms of Co-operation and Communication between Industry and the Universities*. Paris.

O'Toole, J. (1977). *Work, Learning and the American Future*. San Francisco, Jossey-Bass.

Perkin, H. (1984). Historical Perspective, in Clark, B. R. (ed.), *Perspectives on Higher Education: eight disciplinary and comparative views*. San Francisco, University of California Press.

Peters, R. S. (1973). The Justification of Education, in Peters, R. S. (ed.), *The Philosophy of Education*. London, Oxford University Press.

Pippard, A. B. (1972). The Structure of a Morally Committed University, in Lawlor, J. (ed.), *Higher Education: patterns of change in the 1970s*. London, Routledge and Kegan Paul.

Pippard, A. B. *et al.* (1982). The Curriculum of Higher Education in Bligh, D. (ed.), *Professionalism and Flexibility in Learning*, Leverhulme Programme of Study into the Future of Higher Education. Guildford, Society for Research into Higher Education.

Polanyi, M. (1957). Problem-solving, *British Journ. of Philosophy of Science*, Vol. VIII. London.

Popper, K. R. (1969). *Conjectures and Refutations: the growth of scientific knowledge*. London, Routledge and Kegan Paul.

Popper, K. R. (1972). *Objective Knowledge*. London, Oxford University Press.

Robbins Report (1963). *Higher Education*. London, HMSO.

Rose, S. (1986). A Vision out of Focus, *The Times Higher Educational Supplement*. London.

Royal Society of Arts (1987). *Education for Capability and Competence*. London, RSA.

Ryle, G. (1949). *The Concept of the Mind*. London, Hutchinson.

Scheffler, I. (1965). *Conditions of Knowledge*. Chicago, Scott Foresmann.

Schon, D. A. (1971). *Beyond the Stable State*. London, Norton.

Schon, D. A. (1983). *The Reflective Practitioner*. London, Smith.

Schon, D. A. (1984). The Crisis of Professional Knowledge and the Pursuit of an Epistemology of Practice, a paper for the Harvard Business School, 75th Anniversary Colloquium on Teaching by the Case Method. Cambridge, Mass.
 – See also Argyris, C. and Schon, D.

Scott, P. (1984). *The Crisis in the University*. London, Croom Helm.

Select Committee on Education, Sciences and the Arts (1979–80). *Fifth Report: The Funding and Organization of Courses in Higher Education*. House of Commons.

SERC (1985). *Corporate Plan*. Swindon, HMSO.

Shattock, M. (1983). (ed.) *The Structure and Governance of Higher Education*. Leverhulme Programme of Study into the Future of Higher Education, Vol. 9. Guildford, Society for Research into Higher Education.

Shils, E. (1949). Foreword to Weber, M. *Methodology of the Social Sciences*. New York, Free Press.

Shils, E. (1984). *The Academic Ethic*. Chicago, University of Chicago Press.

Sibley, J. (1978). Faculty of Health Sciences, McMaster University, Ontario, Canada – the 1977 Perspective, *Medical Education*.

Smelser, N. (1973). Epilogue in Parsons, T. and Platt, G. *The American University*. Cambridge, Mass., Harvard University Press.

Smith, A. M. (1974). *Many Arts, Many Skills: the polytechnic policy and requirements for its fulfillment*. London, CDP.

Snow, C. P. (1961). *The Two Cultures and the Scientific Revolution*. Cambridge, Cambridge University Press.

Snyder, B. (1971). *The Hidden Curriculum*. Cambridge, Mass, MIT Press.

Society for Research in Higher Education (1983). *Excellence in Diversity: towards a new strategy for higher education*. Leverhulme Programme of Study into the Future of Higher Education. Guildford, Society for Research into Higher Education.

UGC (1984). *A Strategy for Higher Education in the 1990s*. London, HMSO.

University of Warwick (1986). *Annual Report*. Coventry.

Volpe, R. (1981). Knowledge from Theory and Practice, *Oxford Rev. of Ed.*, Vol 7. Oxford.

Wagner, L. (1982). The Challenge of Change in Wagner, L. (ed.), *Agenda for Institutional Change in Higher Education*. Leverhulme Programme of Study into the Future of Higher Education, Vol. 3. Guildford, Society for Research into Higher Education.

Whitehead, A. N. (1932). *The Aims of Education*. London, Williams and Norgate.

Williams, G. and Blackstone, T. (1983). *Response to Adversity*. Leverhulme Programme of Study into the Future of Higher Education, Vol. 10. Guildford, Society for Research into Higher Education.

Index

The Society for Research Into Higher Education

The Society exists both to encourage and to co-ordinate research and development into all aspects of higher education, including academic, organizational and policy issues; and also to provide a forum for debate, verbal and printed. Through its activities, it draws attention to the significance of research into, and development in, higher education and to the needs of scholars in this field. (It is not concerned with research generally, except, for instance, as a subject of study.)

The Society's income is derived from its subscriptions, book sales, conferences and specific grants. It is wholly independent. Its corporate members are institutions of higher education, research institutions and professional, industrial, and governmental bodies. Its individual members include teachers and researchers, administrators and students. Members are found in all parts of the world and the society regards its international work as among its most important activities.

The Society discusses and comments on policy, organizes conferences and encourages research. Under the Imprint SHRE & OPEN UNIVERSITY PRESS, it is a specialist publisher, having some 40 titles in print. It also publishes *Studies in Higher Education* (three times a year) which is mainly concerned with academic issues, *Higher Education Quarterly* (formerly *Universities Quarterly*) which will be mainly concerned with policy issues, *Research into Higher Education Abstracts* (three times a year), and a *Bulletin* (six times a year).

The Society's committees, study groups and branches are run by members (with help from a small staff at Guildford), and aim to provide a form for discussion. The groups at present include a Teacher Education Study Group, a Staff Development Group, a Women in Higher Education Group and a Continuing Education Group which may have had their own organization, subscriptions or publications; (eg the *Staff Development Newsletter*). The Governing Council, elected by members, comments on current issues; and discusses policies with leading figures, notably at its evening Forums. The Society organizes seminars on current research for officials of DES and other ministries, an Anglo-American series on standards, and is in touch with bodies in the UK such as the NAB, CVCP, UGC, CNAA and the British Council, and with sister-bodies overseas. Its current research projects include one on the relationship between entry qualifications and degree results, directed by Prof. W.

D. Furneaux (Brunel) and one on questions of quality directed by Prof. G. C. Moodie (York). A project on the evaluation of the research standing of university departments is in preparation. The Society's conferences are often held jointly. Annual Conferences have considered 'Professional Education' (1984), 'Continuing Education' (1985, with Goldsmiths' College), 'Standards and Criteria in Higher Education' (1986, with Bulmershe CHE), 'Restructuring' (1987, with the City of Birmingham Polytechnic) and 'Academic Freedom' (1988, the University of Surrey). Other conferences have considered the DES 'Green Paper' (1985, with the Times Higher Education Supplement), and 'The First-Year Experience' (1986, with the University of South Carolina and Newcastle Polytechnic). For some of the Society's conferences, special studies are commissioned in advance, as 'Precedings'.

Members receive free of charge the Society's *Abstracts*, annual conference Proceedings (or 'Precedings'), *Bulletin and International Newsletter* and may buy SHRE & OPEN UNIVERSITY PRESS books at booksellers' discount. Corporate members also receive the Society's journal *Studies in Higher Education* free (individuals at a heavy discount). They may also obtain *Evaluation Newsletter* and certain other journals at a discount, including the NFER *Register of Educational Research*. There is a substantial discount to members, and to staff of corporate members, on annual and some other conference fees.